TOWARDS A SCIENCE OF TEACHING

towards a science of
TEACHING

Edited by Gabriel Chanan

National Foundation for Educational Research

NFER Publishing Company Limited

Published by the NFER Publishing Company Ltd.,
Book Division, 2 Jennings Buildings, Thames Avenue,
Windsor, Berks., SL4 1QS
Registered Office, The Mere, Upton Park, Slough, Bucks., SL1 2DQ
First Published 1973
© NFER Publishing Company Ltd., 1973
85633 001 9

Printed in Great Britain by
KING, THORNE & STACE LTD., SCHOOL ROAD, HOVE, BN3 5JE

Distributed in the USA by Fernhill House, Humanities Press Inc.,
450 Park Avenue South, New York, N.Y. 10016, USA.

Contents

Preface

The study of 'classroom interaction' has been going on for some time in America and elsewhere. In this country, attention has only recently been turned towards it. The present book has the dual purpose of fostering the subject among British readers and disseminating important new findings which will be of interest both here and abroad.

It is surprising that we have neglected this topic for so long. 'Classroom interaction' means all that is communicated in the classroom—principally, but not solely, verbal communication. Since talking is such a crucial part of teaching and learning it would seem impossible to have any serious view of either activity which did not make the handling of language in the classroom a central issue. It seems amazing now that whole waves of educational opinion have come and gone without any close look at, for example, the respective ratios of talk by teachers and pupils.

Once we have clearly focused—as the studies in this book will help us do—on the specific ways of asking questions, acknowledging responses, expressing assessments and so forth which are at the teacher's disposal, we are liable to feel that any educational theory which does not take these into account is intolerably vague. Does it make sense to talk of 'child-centred teaching' without specifying in some detail what opportunities for pupil initiative in classroom intercourse are implied in this, and looking at whether these opportunities really exist? Can one be concerned with how teachers' expectations of different pupils influence their attainments and yet not be concerned with the specific kinds of praise, blame, encouragement and discouragement that are embodied in the teacher's statements to the pupils?

No-one would wish to suggest that teaching consists, or should consist, exclusively of talk, even if a large proportion of this were to be pupil talk (a situation which is by no means common even now). Yet it will never be possible to divorce skill in teaching from skill in communicating—in peculiarly difficult circumstances—nor communication from talking. Some of the subtlest qualities of good teaching will always elude research; but the study of classroom interaction is still a great deal closer to them than are those researches which are concerned predominantly with large organizational variables or with very generalized attitudes. If the training of teachers is ever to become a genuinely rational activity, it must surely become much more intimate with the close texture of confrontation between teacher and taught. A particular value of the best researches in this field is that even where they are not wholly conclusive they are of direct practical use to teachers in that they present a schema of the various ways in which lessons may be structured and different teaching 'components' weighted.

This much from the point of view of teaching and teacher education. But the field has other aspects and other applications. It is not only largely by talking that the teacher teaches, but by talking that the learner learns. Classroom interaction is concerned with more than what the teacher should say and how he should say it. It is potentially concerned with the whole function of language in the development of the child.

This potentiality, admittedly, has not yet been more than marginally realized. Classroom interaction studies so far have tended to focus on the teacher's verbal behaviour very much more than on the children's. In part this is because of the preponderance of teacher talk over pupil talk—a disturbing fact revealed by these very studies. But in part one may wonder whether some of the researches do not inadvertently reinforce an assumption of a teacher-directed norm for classroom talk. The teacher has the initiative, the teacher solicits responses, the teacher rewards or criticizes those responses. As writers on language development have noted, the form of these recurrent transactions frequently represents a very narrow understanding on the teacher's part of the function of the pupil's own use of language in the learning process—a preoccupation with getting the children to slot in phraseologically limited 'right answers' preconceived by the teacher, rather than with getting the children to use language to develop their own thought processes. The most fruitful direction of classroom research may be one which, in the light of its own revelations about the preponderance of teacher talk and its dominant patterns, now turns as keen a spotlight on the nature and function of pupils' own talk.

G. Chanan,
Editor, NFER.

Experimental Studies of Teaching Behaviour

Graham Nuthall and John Church
University of Canterbury, Christchurch, New Zealand

Research on classroom teaching has a long, spasmodic and largely unsuccessful history. While early experimental psychologists such as Thorndike (1906) advocated the need for experimental research on teaching methods, and early psychological theorists such as Watson (1913) held high hopes for the future of experimental pedagogy, research on teaching has never been the object of consistent interest or systematic development. There are virtually no books about empirical research on teaching which do other than report particular research studies. We remain very largely ignorant of how teachers affect the intellectual and emotional development of the pupils they teach, and, more significantly, we remain very largely ignorant of how best to go about developing this knowledge.

Recent years have seen a renewed interest in the development of empirical knowledge about teaching and in the development of category systems designed for the observation and analysis of teacher-pupil interaction. The pioneering research of Jayne (1945), Flanders (1960) and Smith (1961) has led to a proliferation of studies involving the collection of observational data from school classrooms.

We now know a great deal about the range of different behaviours and behaviour-styles which can be observed in an average classroom. But data-gathering alone is not enough. A good deal of the research has been motivated by the hope that systematic classroom observation and interaction analysis will provide the key that is needed to unlock the mysteries of teaching. It is hoped that vague generalizations about teaching methods can be replaced by precisely quantified descriptions, and that the new observational category systems will play the same role in the development of a science of teaching as the telescope and the microscope have played in the development of the physical and biological sciences.

Now that the first flush of enthusiasm for observing classroom interaction is over, and we have an encyclopaedic catalogue of observation systems (Simon and Boyer, 1967) available for handy reference, it is becoming clear that very few writers have paid any attention to what the next stages in research on teaching might be.

If we are to develop a scientific understanding of the teaching process, what kind of knowledge do we require? If teachers are to make use of findings from empirical research on teaching, what kinds of findings will be most useful? We know that we can obtain reliable observational data on teacher-pupil interaction. We now know that attempts to identify the personality of the ideal teacher, and studies comparing popular teaching methods have been fruitless endeavours. But we do not know what kinds of research procedures will lead us from simple observational studies towards an effective and useful psychological understanding of the teaching process.

The studies reported in this article were intended to explore the possibility of conducting controlled experimental studies of teaching in a normal classroom context. They were designed to provide information about how such studies could be carried out and to provide a sample of the kind of data which such studies might produce.

This article does not provide a detailed analysis of the empirical data obtained from these studies. Such an analysis is well beyond the scope of this article. Instead we have attempted to describe the nature of the studies, to make explicit the assumptions and reasons that shaped the direction of the research, and to give a general overview of the empirical data which have been obtained from this research.

If the reader can obtain some insight into the problems involved in obtaining reliable empirical knowledge about classroom learning, and get some feeling for what it could mean to develop a scientific understanding of teaching, then this article will have served its purpose.

It is clear that developing an adequate understanding of the psychological nature of teaching is going to require an enormous expenditure of time and effort in painstaking research activities. To date we have never expended this kind of systematic and directed research effort in any area in education. If research on teaching is worth pursuing then we must be sure we know which way to go and how to get there. We need discussion of the alternative research strategies which are available. This article is intended to provide a basis on which such a discussion might take place.

The article is divided into three sections. First, we deal with the beliefs and assumptions which have guided our research. Second, we deal with the empirical background of the studies and the kinds of teacher behaviour variables with which we have been concerned. In the final section the experimental studies are described and the data presented.

I   BELIEFS AND ASSUMPTIONS UNDERLYING THE RESEARCH

(a) The purpose of the studies

The major belief which has guided our research is the belief that classroom teaching is worth studying, as it exists, for its own sake. Many of those interested in classroom inter-action studies have been primarily motivated by the desire to improve existing practice by replacing it with some more desirable alternative. Frequently they have come to this kind of research with the conviction that teaching needs to be changed, and that research on teaching will provide the data to convince others of this need.

While we have a deep-felt concern for the improvement of teaching, we have attempted not to let this concern distort the nature of our research. In the long run, the interests of education are best served by developing a comprehensive understanding of classroom teaching, rather than by finding immediate solutions to topical questions. The practice of teaching in most Western countries is a relatively stable, self-contained and repetitive set of behaviours. It recurs daily, in much the same way, in thousands of different classrooms. However good or bad the teaching might be, it has the kind of regularity which makes it an ideal object for systematic behavioural analysis. Our hope has been to undertake a *psychological* study of classroom behaviour which moves towards an understanding of it, without prejudging the issue as to whether or not it ought to be changed. The important questions are: how do pupils learn in classrooms? and how are observable teacher behaviours related to that learning?

(b) The nature of the data

The second point that needs to be made is that we have a rather different view of the kinds of variables that are significant in teaching research from many other investigators in the field. Working primarily from a background in the psychology of learning, we have been concerned with teaching behaviour rather than with teacher characteristics. Our interest has been with those particular behaviours of which teachers are conscious, and which they can learn to manipulate. Our analysis is a fine-grain analysis, dealing with the moment-by-moment chaining of teacher and pupil acts.

It is our hope that we will come to understand teaching in terms of those behaviours which can readily be observed and learned by teachers-in-training.

(c) The nature of the scientific enterprise

Thirdly, we have been guided, so far as possible, by an idealized view of how a field of empirical investigation ought to be developed. We would hope to see it operating through a four stage cycle.

The *first* stage is one in which the phenomenon being investigated is approached descriptively. Observers sit in classrooms, becoming familiar with the phenomenon, and developing ways of categorizing the behaviour. (Nuthall and Lawrence, 1965.)

The *second* stage is one in which an attempt is made to find inter-relationships between behaviour variables observed in natural classroom situations and measures of student learning. The studies involved are correlational studies, and the object of them is to indicate the relative significance of the descriptive categories which have been developed in the first stage. Correlational studies provide the kind of evidence which is needed to determine which kinds of behaviours are worth investigating further, and which kinds of behaviours are probably irrelevant. (Wright and Nuthall, 1970.)

The *third* stage is one in which an attempt is made to provide experimental validation of the relationships suggested in the correlational studies. An experimental study is one in which behaviour variables are manipulated in such a way that the effects of this manipulation can be observed on other behaviours, and on changes in pupil learning.

Each of these latter two stages feeds information both forwards and backwards. Descriptive studies provide the background for correlational and experimental studies. But it is equally important that results of correlational and experimental studies should be used to refine and develop descriptive categories and suggest new observational studies. For instance, a good correlational study should suggest the need for further descriptive studies in which new variables are observed, or old variables are looked at in new ways.

Constant interaction between the first three stages should lead inevitably to the fourth stage. In this final stage explanatory theory is developed which accounts for the relationships uncovered in the experimental studies. This theory becomes embodied in the descriptive system, so that the variables which have proved significant in the correlational and experimental studies can be identified by any user of the descriptive system.

This is the idealized set of procedures which we have taken as our model. It is our hope that this set of procedures will produce a workable theory of classroom teaching and learning which is closely tied to the observable behaviours of the classroom. Deducing practical application from such a theory should then be a relatively simple procedure.

(b)   **The effects of this research model**
      There are a number of consequences of following a model of this kind, of which we have become aware as we have proceeded. Two of these are worth mentioning at this point:
      (i)   The price you pay for pursuing a particular line of research is that you come to narrow your view of the data. Our search has necessarily been a search for variables which are controllable, and for relationships which appear to be relatively stable. We have had to drop our interest in aspects of classroom behaviour, and of pupil learning, which could not be brought under some kind of experimental control.
      For instance, we have concerned ourselves with the measurement of those aspects of pupil learning which can be related directly to the content of lessons, because other aspects of learning are difficult to measure, require an enormous expenditure of time and effort in test development, and cannot be clearly related to classroom events. We have looked only at those teacher behaviours which can be varied systematically without complete loss of control of the general direction of a lesson. It is clearly not possible to experiment with situations in which individual pupils exercise a large measure of control over their own experiences.
      The effect is that our experimental studies will look excessively narrow in their orientation to those who are concerned with other kinds of pupil learning, and other kinds of teaching. But, we make no apology. It is the price that needs to be paid to produce sound, replicable empirical data. At this stage in the development of research on teaching, the major problem is to identify *any* reliable empirical relationships without being over-concerned with the quality of those relationships.
      (ii)   Secondly, as a consequence of trying to let the data speak for themselves, we have had to keep our thinking open about ways of conceptualizing variables and relationships between variables.
      For instance, we have been forced to cope with the fact that many classroom behaviour variables are reciprocally related to each other. You just cannot hope to conduct a series of experiments in which you vary one variable at a time, independently of all the others. For example, if you change the nature of teacher questions, you also affect the nature of pupil responses, the kinds of feedback which a teacher will need to use, the time taken to cover a particular unit of content, and so on.

II   THE DESCRIPTIVE ANALYSIS SYSTEM

Discussion of the experimental studies requires some preliminary familiarization with the behavioural concepts and terms that have evolved from our work. Our concern is primarily with the discussion-type of lesson in which teachers and pupils interact verbally, and in which the object of that interaction is some relatively self-contained unit of subject matter. This is clearly not the only kind of teaching which takes place in classrooms but, in the upper elementary level where we have done most of our work, it is certainly the most common.

The first point to bear in mind in understanding this analysis system is that there are two conceptually distinguishable dimensions to verbal interaction in discussion-type lessons. The *first* dimension is the content or meaning dimension. Teacher and pupils are talking about subject matter. In a general sense, content is being 'covered'. The *second* dimension is the dimension of inter-personal control. The teacher's verbal behaviour is guiding and controlling the verbal participation of the pupils (and vice versa).

These two dimensions are closely intertwined with each other, so that most verbal behaviours have both a function in relation to the content (i.e. they have content meaning), and also a function in the control of the interaction which takes place. It would be elegant to be able to separate these two dimensions and deal with them independently, but we have not found this possible. For instance, one of the most important teacher behaviours is the asking of questions. In classroom verbal interaction, the question functions to elicit pupil responses. It is the teacher's primary means of inducing pupil participation. The question also has meaning with reference to the subject-matter, so that it determines the content of the elicited response. Variations in teacher questions affect both the way the subject-matter is handled, and the nature of pupil participation. Generally speaking, if you manipulate the nature of teacher questions, you manipulate both the way subject-matter is dealt with, and the way in which pupils participate.

Most teacher verbal behaviours have this dual function, although there are some which appear to have only a single function. For instance: a reprimand from a teacher ('pay attention!') appears to have only a controlling function, and a lecture appears to have only a subject-matter function.

(a) Verbal moves and episodes

Because we have been impressed with the functional significance of teacher questions, these questions form the central point of our descriptive analysis.

The basic unit of the analysis is the *verbal move*. A verbal move is a unit of discourse which has a single identifiable verbal function (in either the control or content dimensions). For instance: a teacher question is a verbal move, a pupil response to a question is another kind of verbal move, a teacher comment on a pupil response is a further kind of verbal move, and so on.

During class discussions, verbal moves occur in interdependent clusters, which we call *episodes*. An episode consists of a single content-oriented teacher question, and all of the verbal moves made by teacher and pupils which are associated directly with that question. The episode is an easily recognized unit of discussion, which has been identified in the work of several different investigators. Figure 1 contains a typical example.

b) Major types and patterns of verbal moves

A list of the major types of verbal moves of which we have made use in our experimental studies is included in the key to Figure 2. The complete set which we use in the analysis of transcripts is considerably more extensive, and has been reported elsewhere (Nuthall, *et al.*, 1970.)

The basic kind of episode consists of a teacher question (1), followed by an acceptable pupil response (6.1), which is then followed by some kind of teacher comment (3). If the pupils cannot give an immediate acceptable response, or the teacher wishes to involve more than one pupil, or the teacher wishes to digress, etc., then further kinds of verbal moves get included in the episode. The number of different kinds of episodes which can be observed is very large, but the sequencing of moves does appear to follow established patterns.

Figure 1: *An episode occurring in a high school literature class*

		Type of Move*
Teacher:	It looks as if he's taken his picture and now he's going to put in a little lesson for us. Can you see it in the last verse? A change? He's no longer describing the bugle—he's drawing a lesson for us. *What's the lesson?*—in your opinion, what is implied in the author's words?	3.1
		1.1
Student:	Our echoes roll from soul to soul.	6
Teacher:	What does that mean?	5.3
Student:	Getting ready to depart our life.	6
Teacher:	You're getting nearer to it now.	4.3
Student:	You die like the echoes.	6
Teacher:	Our echoes—what are these?	5.3
Student:	You'd think some remember us after death, but they don't. They might on our anniversary or that, but they forget.	6
Teacher:	But he says they grow forever.	3.2
	What are these echoes?	5.1
Student:	If you do a great work like a poet you die, but you're remembered for it.	6
Teacher:	Could be like a poet who is often better known after death. 'Nobody's any good until they're dead.' (Laughter round class.)	3.2
Student:	You may be forgotten, but you're rewarded in heaven.	6
Teacher:	Yes, it could be that, but I'm inclined to think it's something different.	4.3
	Our echoes roll . . . forever.	3.2
Student:	Words go far.	6
Teacher:	You're getting near it now.	4.3
Student:	Our good deeds.	6
Teacher:	Yes, the things we do—you have an influence on him, he has an influence on him, and so on and on (etc.).	3.3

*See Key to Figure 2.

Figure 2 contains a schematic representation of the most common sequences of moves in an episode. Address moves (naming pupils to respond) have been omitted to simplify the diagram although they do have considerable functional significance in the management of discussion.

III   THE EXPERIMENTAL STUDIES

(a)   Teacher intentions

In a correlational study reported elsewhere (Wright and Nuthall, 1970) a group of 17 teachers was asked to teach a specified topic over a series of three lessons in normal class-room conditions. The teachers were left free to present the material in any way they thought appropriate. Data obtained from analysis of audio-recordings of the lessons indicated that

Figure 2: *Flow-chart of common verbal move sequences in an episode*

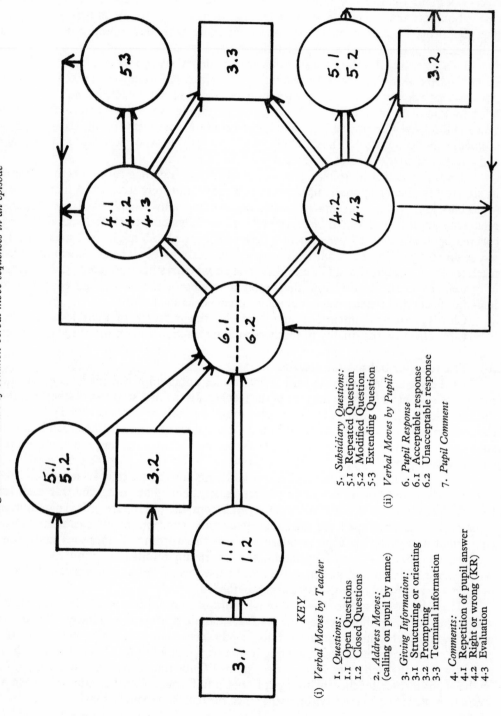

KEY

(i) *Verbal Moves by Teacher*

1. *Questions:*
   1.1 Open Questions
   1.2 Closed Questions

2. *Address Moves:*
   (calling on pupil by name)

3. *Giving Information:*
   3.1 Structuring or orienting
   3.2 Prompting
   3.3 Terminal information

4. *Comments:*
   4.1 Repetition of pupil answer
   4.2 Right or wrong (KR)
   4.3 Evaluation

5. *Subsidiary Questions:*
   5.1 Repeated Question
   5.2 Modified Question
   5.3 Extending Question

(ii) *Verbal Moves by Pupils*

6. *Pupil Response*
   6.1 Acceptable response
   6.2 Unacceptable response

7. *Pupil Comment*

the more experienced teachers made use of relatively more open-ended (higher cognitive level) questions than less experienced teachers. Since the data also indicated a negative correlation between the use of open-ended questions and pupil learning, it was suggested that experienced teachers might be concerned more with developing intellectual skills rather than with the direct learning of subject-matter content.

This latter hypothesis was tested in an experimental study reported by Francis (1971). Eight teachers were asked to teach two topics to their classes. They were asked to teach one topic so that the pupils would 'learn and remember the new material', and to teach the other to 'stimulate the children's ability to think'. Pupils were given two pretests (intelligence and logical thinking ability) and three criterion post-tests (recall, recognition, and problem solving transfer). The teaching of the topics was tape recorded, and 23 teacher and pupil behaviour variables abstracted from the transcripts.

It was found that in 'thinking' lessons, pupils used more logical connectives (because, if, so, etc.) in their responses, teachers talked proportionately less, asked more questions (especially higher-level questions), used more probing moves, and asked more questions related to pupil responses. In 'achievement-oriented' lessons, teachers lectured more and covered approximately 18 per cent more relevant content. As might be expected, pupils' scores on recognition and recall tests were significantly higher when teachers intended to teach for learning, but this difference disappeared when results were corrected for amount of content covered. Results from the problem-solving criterion test showed a slight but non-significant difference in favour of achievement-oriented lessons.

Clearly, teachers' intentions in relation to the outcome of their lessons have an observable effect on the quality of teacher-pupil interaction and on measured outcomes.

(b)   The teacher behaviour studies

In the second and third experimental studies an attempt was made to obtain much more precise control of the behaviour of the teacher. In the first study on teacher intentions, the variable under scrutiny was not a behavioural variable and it was sufficient to involve the co-operation of teachers working in their normal classrooms. In the second and third studies, the variables examined were specific teacher behaviours, and much more precise control was required.

This was achieved by developing lesson-scripts for the series of lessons used in each of the studies, and having the same person (experimenter) act as teacher for each set of lessons. An example of a short section of script is contained in Figure 3. It is a section from a set of lessons developed for teaching elementary concepts about electricity. Display equipment and materials were standardized and the wording of questions and prompts was predetermined. For each question, the maximum number of pupil responses and the points at which prompting moves might be used was fixed. A summary of the content to be covered by pupil responses was also provided.

Thus the lesson script consisted of a set of question-initiated episodes (see Figure 2) with predetermined rules guiding the teacher's handling of pupil responses. These scripts were developed through a series of trials in pilot classrooms until they could be used to produce an effective and smooth flowing lesson with characteristics very similar to lessons taken by average teachers in average classrooms.[1] Once the script was thoroughly learned by the experimenter-teacher, neither pupils nor uninformed observers appear to have been aware that the lessons were anything other than normal classroom lessons.

[1]For one of the studies, the scripts were modelled on transcripts of teachers teaching the same material to their own classes in any way which they thought most appropriate.

Figure 3: *Extract from typical lesson script*

DISPLAYS CARD 3:10 WHICH SHOWS:
(A) ELECTROMAGNET AND OPEN SWITCH,
(B) BULB AND OPEN SWITCH,
IN PARALLEL ACROSS TWO CELLS IN SERIES.
What would happen if we connected these up?
NUMBER OF RESPONSES: 2
Could we make the bulb work?
NUMBER OF RESPONSES: 2
PROMPT: What exactly must we do to make just the bulb shine?
TO COVER: Close *only* switch B to make the complete path through the bulb.
Now, who can still remember the closed circuit rule?
NUMBER OF RESPONSES: 3
DISPLAYS TELEPHONE GENERATOR WITH LEAD TO ONE SIDE OF THE BULB
DISCONNECTED.
What do we have to do to get the current flowing?
NUMBER OF RESPONSES: 1
Well, why isn't it working?
NUMBER OF RESPONSES: 4
PROMPT: We have to turn the coil round alright, but we have to do something else as well.
PROMPT: Into what kind of circuit?
TO COVER: Coil must be connected into a closed circuit as well as being turned around.

To achieve an additional measure of control, all lessons were tape-recorded, trans-cribed and subjected to a detailed behavioural analysis. A selection of some of the behaviour measures obtained from recordings made of lessons taken in four different classrooms by the same experimenter-teacher using the same script is contained in Table 1. It can be seen that while there is a great deal of uniformity between these four replications of the same lessons (the content covered is exactly the same) there is also some variation which must be taken into account in the final analysis of the results obtained from these lessons. For instance, the proportion of correct responses made by pupils in Class 40 is somewhat higher and there is a consequent decrease in the relative total number of subsidiary questions.

Table 1: *Selection of data obtained from recording of lessons taken in four different classrooms from the same script*

| Variable | Classroom Number | | | |
(Total for two-lesson sequence)	29	31	34	40
Time (minutes)	71	72	68	71
Episodes	108	107	111	110
Teacher:				
KR moves	104	104	116	121
Prompting moves	13	19	18	16
Total Subsidiary Questions	73	88	81	64
Terminal Informing moves	17	22	15	16
Pupils:				
Accepted Responses	124	117	123	135
Unaccepted Responses	26	39	33	14
Unjudged Responses	32	39	36	24

(i)   *Varying the address of questions*

In the correlational study reported by Wright and Nuthall (1970), there appeared to be a significant relationship between pupil learning and the way in which teachers directed questions around the class. It seemed probable that different patterns of directing questions affected pupil attention in some way which was unrelated to differences in pupil participation.

In order to investigate this hypothesis, a set of experimental studies was designed in which the major variable was the pattern of directing questions (Hughes, 1971). A set of three 35-minute lessons on game animals in New Zealand was scripted in the manner described above. Three classes of average ability pupils were selected from each of three Intermediate Schools (average pupil age 12 to 13 years). All the children were pretested on a series of ability, attitude and achievement tests. The set of three scripted lessons was taken by the same experimenter-teacher with each of the classes. At the beginning of the week immediately following the teaching, each class was given a series of criterion tests measuring knowledge of the information and principles contained in the lessons and ability to use the principles taught with new material.

First Treatment. In three classes (one from each school) questions were addressed at random around the class, with each pupil being called on an equal number of times.

Second Treatment. In another three classes, questions were addressed to pupils in a preplanned systematic fashion. Pupils were informed that, in order to give all an equal chance of participating, questions would be asked of all pupils in order of seating position from one side of the class to the other.

Third Treatment. In the final three classes, pupils who wanted to answer questions were asked to raise their hands in the usual manner. Only those pupils who volunteered were ever asked to answer any question.

It was thought that when pupils were aware that questions would be directed in a sequential fashion around the class, they could be certain of having to pay attention only at certain predictable times. Between the occasions when their turn came around, they could let their attention wander. On the other hand, when questions were directed in an unpredictable random manner, pupils would feel constrained to pay attention all the time. The procedure of letting pupils volunteer to answer questions should result in some pupils volunteering and paying attention a great deal of the time, and others remaining uninvolved.

Analysis of the data indicated that pupil learning (criterion test performance corrected for ability, attitude and prior achievement) was unrelated to these variations in the address of questions. Even when a detailed analysis was made comparing pupils who volunteered frequently with pupils who never volunteered within classes given the third treatment, no differences in learning could be detected.

A second experiment in this study was undertaken to see if frequency of teacher reaction to pupil responses was a critical variable. Being asked to answer a question involves not only a pupil response but also a reaction or comment on that response from the teacher.

In this second experiment, two similar classes were selected and the pupils in each class divided into two randomly selected halves. One half of each class was labelled the Reaction group and the other half the No-Reaction group. The same lessons were taught as those used in the first experiment with random direction of questions around the class. The teacher reacted to the answers given by the pupils in the No-Reaction group by merely repeating or stating the correct answers. The responses given by pupils in the Reaction group were given appropriate praise or supportive correction, with occasional urging and reproof if called for. In other words the teacher responded actively and individually to the pupils in the Reaction group, and entirely neutrally to pupils in the No-Reaction group.

Analysis of the data obtained from this experiment indicated a significant improvement in learning for the Reaction group. This improvement was greatest on content covered in the last lesson, so that it appears to have been a cumulative effect.

The results from these experiments and other related research seem to indicate that pupil participation is not closely related to pupil learning, nor is it related to pupils' expectations about having to answer questions. If pupil attention is important, it must be related more to the nature of teacher reactions to individual pupil answers than to the way the teacher directs questions around the class.

(ii) *Varying the nature of teacher questions and comments*

The third experimental study[1] involved a more elaborate and extensive design. It was apparent that a systematic exploration of the complexities of teaching behaviours required a situation in which multiple comparisons between a series of experimental treatments was possible. Traditional experimental designs such as factorial designs involving analysis of variance procedures presume that experimental variables can be isolated and manipulated independently of each other. They also presume that the experimental results can be meaningfully expressed in terms of levels of statistical significance. The experimental treatments described below were designed in such a way that they form a cumulative set. The results obtained from any one particular treatment can be evaluated by comparison with the results obtained from any other particular treatment.

Lesson scripts and display materials designed to introduce the principles of elementary electricity to ten-year-old children were developed in the manner described above. For each experimental treatment a different script was prepared which varied from the scripts for other treatments in some specified manner. A summary description of each of the treatments is contained in Table 2.

The first three treatments (A, B and C) were developed as standard treatments in which the only variation was the thoroughness with which the content was covered. They range from one treatment (A) in which all the necessary content was covered briefly in one 50-minute period, to the third standard treatment in which the *same* content was expanded, repeated, and reviewed to fill up three 40-minute lessons. The results obtained from these treatments were intended to provide a set of standard levels of pupil learning against which treatments involving variations in teacher behaviours could be evaluated.

The remaining treatments involved variation in specified teacher behaviours. Treatments D, E and F each involved changing highly structured, closed questions into more open and unstructured questions. Since open questions lead to more incomplete or incorrect pupil responses, there was a need for teacher strategies which helped pupils toward the required answers. There are at least three possibilities: the teacher may close discussion by giving the required information (Treatment D), by letting the discussion go on longer and involving more and more pupils until the required information is obtained (Treatment E) or by providing the pupils with additional prompts or clues to help them work out the information for themselves (Treatment F).

The remaining three treatments involved replacing questioning by direct informing (Treatment G), reducing pupil opportunity to participate (Treatment H) and reducing the frequency of feedback comments (Treatment I).

[1]This research was partly financed by the McKenzie Foundation. The assistance of this foundation is gratefully acknowledged.

Each treatment was replicated in at least three different classes. All classes involved were at the New Zealand Standard Four level (10-year-old children). The procedure for each class was as follows. All the children were pretested several weeks before the treatment, and a criterion post-test of knowledge and application of the concepts and principles taught in the lessons was administered four days (including a weekend) after the last lesson.

One of the major problems involved in using normal classes in schools is that children may vary greatly in background and ability from school to school. Analysis of covariance techniques (used in the second study described above) can provide some correction of prior differences, but they are not a completely adequate solution to the problem, (see for example Lord, 1969). It was decided in this series of experiments to identify those pupils

Table 2: *Abbreviated descriptions of experimental treatments*

Treatment:

A. *Single Standard:* Covers as briefly as possible post-test content, using highly structured closed questions. Single reference is made to each concept name, concept definition, concept example, and principle. Reference is made to two problems illustrating each of the three principles. One 50-minute lesson, 54 episodes. Questions addressed by random non-replacement procedure, average of five responses per pupil.

B. *Double Standard:* Same procedure as for Single Standard, but content is doubled, i.e. two references to each concept name, definition, example, and each principle. Four references to problems illustrating each principle. Two 35-minute lessons, 111 episodes. Questions addressed by random non-replacement procedure, average of nine responses per pupil.

C. *Triple Standard:* Same procedure as Single Standard, but content is tripled, i.e. three references to each concept name, definition, example, and to each principle. Six references to problems illustrating each principle. Three 40-minute lessons, 179 episodes. Questions addressed by random non-replacement procedure, average of 15 responses per pupil.

D. *Open Question: terminal comment:* Same content and number of moves as Double Standard. Questions are opened (less structured, vague) and addressed to pupils who volunteer. Wrong answers handled by redirecting questions to further pupils, and content coverage controlled by terminal information moves (giving answers). Two 35-minute lessons, 86 episodes.

E. *Open Question: evaluation only:* Same content and number of moves as Double Standard. Questions are opened as in above treatment. Wrong answers are handled by redirecting to further pupils, by evaluation, KR, and repetition comments. Number of pupil responses is allowed to increase to level of Triple Standard treatment. Control of length of episodes exercised by directing questions to pupils of differing ability. Three 35-minute lessons, 90 episodes.

F. *Open Question: prompting moves:* Same content and number of episodes as Double Standard. Questions opened as for above treatment. Number of responses as for Triple Standard (see above treatment). Control of content coverage through use of prompting (additional information during episode) moves, and through redirection of questions to pupils of differing ability levels. Three 40-minute lessons, 97 episodes.

G. *Infrequent Questions:* Same content as Triple Standard, number of questions as for Single Standard treatment. Two-thirds of questions in Triple Standard treatment turned into information moves, either structuring or terminal. Three 25-minute lessons, 52 episodes.

H. *Infrequent Responses:* Same content and procedures as for Triple Standard treatment, but almost all questions addressed to non-experimental subjects. Three 40-minute lessons, 180 episodes.

I. *Infrequent Feedback:* Content as for Triple Standard, but number of feedback comments reduced to number as for Single Standard treatment. Pupils were asked to write down answers to two-thirds of questions, and not told whether they were correct. Three 40-minute lessons, 180 episodes.

N. *No Instruction:* Classes which received the same testing programme as other classes but no instruction.

in each class whose ability and prior knowledge fell within an 'average' range. These pupils were treated as the experimental subjects, and others in the class treated as non-experimental subjects. Experimental subjects were defined as those pupils: (a) whose intelligence (measured on Cattell's *Culture Fair Test*) was within the range 90 to 129 IQ points, (b) who scored more than 75 per cent on a pretest of prerequisite knowledge needed to understand and participate in the lessons, and (c) who scored at little more than a chance level on a pretest sampling the content of the lessons.

Many classes were pretested, but only those that included at least 20 pupils who could be classified as experimental subjects (on the above criteria) were included in the experiments. Each class was taught as a whole, but care was taken to address only certain content-irrelevant questions to any non-experimental subjects in the class. The measure of learning used as a criterion measure for each class was the average performance of the experimental subjects on the post-test, corrected for individual differences in ability and prior knowledge. Thus, the results reported in Figure 4 and Table 3 were obtained from approximately comparable 'average' pupils in classes consisting mainly of such pupils.

The results reported in Figure 4 and Table 3 can be interpreted in many different ways depending on the kinds of questions that might be asked.

First, there is the general picture of the data obtained from the full set of experimental lessons. There is a good deal of similarity between the effects of replication of the same treatment in different classes. The control exercised over teaching behaviours within any particular treatment does seem to have been generally effective in controlling measured pupil learning.

Changing the amount of time spent on relevant content (Treatments A, B and C) produces considerably larger changes in achievement than changes in teacher behaviours when the coverage of content is held constant (Treatments D to I). Comparisons made between appropriate groups of treatments suggest that variations in coverage of content may account for 37 per cent of the variance in pupil criterion test achievement, variation in teacher behaviours may account for seven per cent of the total variance, and uncontrolled variations between classes given the same experimental treatment may account for up to three per cent.

Second, information can be obtained about the effects of different teaching behaviours by making particular comparisons between different treatments. The following is a summary of some of the interpretations which are possible from the data.

1 The effects of questions

Treatment G involved the same content as treatment C, with a marked reduction in the number of questions asked and consequently in the number of pupil responses and the time taken. From Figure 4 it is evident that reducing the number of questions by about two-thirds is about equivalent to reducing the content covered by about one third (Treatment B).

It might be argued that this effect is due to the lower number of opportunities for pupils to respond. But consider the effects of reducing the number of pupil responses.

2 Reducing pupil responses

Treatment H involved the same content as treatment C, but with almost all the questions directed to non-experimental subjects. The experimental subjects answered almost no content-relevant questions, but they heard other pupils answering. The effect was a significant lowering of achievement, but the reduction was not as great as the reduction in the case of the no-question treatment. Apparently hearing other pupils answer questions is better than hearing the teacher give the same information directly.

Consider now what happens when the questions the teacher asks are changed so that the kinds of answers required are less definite and more general.

Table 3: *Adjusted mean achievement-test scores*

Treatment:	Class No.	Adjusted Mean	No. of Pupils
N. No Instruction	1	14·90	20
	2	16·34	20
	5	14·04	20
	6	14·25	20
A. Single Standard	33	23·92	20
	35	27·64	20
	36	25·36	17
	42	25·57	20
B. Double Standard	29	30·57	20
	31	31·49	19
	34	31·39	20
	40	31·36	20
C. Triple Standard			
(a) Beginning of year replication	28	38·17	19
	30	36·13	18
	32	34·89	20
(b) End of year replication	58	38·29	19
	60	33·52	20
	62	37·09	18
D. Open Question: terminal comments	41	27·80	19
	46	29·18	17
	51	26·89	19
E. Open Question: evaluation only	43	27·98	16
	47	28·41	17
	48	32·23	20
	55	26·55	16
F. Open Question: prompting moves	39	31·02	19
	45	31·02	14
	49	32·42	18
	52	31·13	15
G. Infrequent Questions	44	34·01	16
	57	32·67	15
	59	29·33	19
H. Infrequent Responses	54	33·21	16
	64	33·89	19
	65	32·29	19
I. Infrequent Feedback	53	29·72	18
	61	29·67	18
	63	31·18	18

Figure 4: *The effects of experimental treatments on pupil achievement*

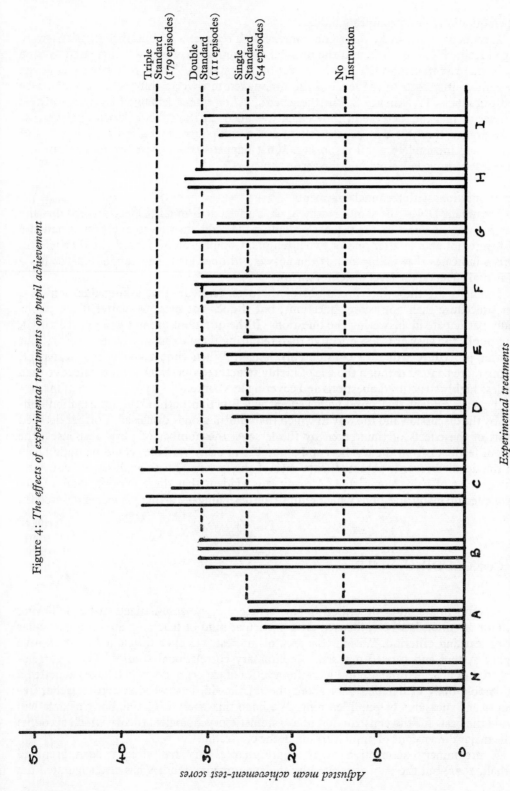

Experimental treatments

(Each line in the graph represents the average score obtained from one class)

3 Open questions with prompting moves

Treatment F involved the same content as Treatment B, but the questions were changed from closed to open, and the number of prompting moves was increased to cope with the increase in incomplete and incorrect pupil responses. The time taken to cover the same content increased to the level of the time taken to cover a third more content with closed questions (Treatment C), but the level of achievement remained constant. In this case it seems that the increase in time taken was offset by the effect of open questions. It may be argued that this was because there was a consequent increase in the number of incorrect and incomplete pupil responses. What happens when these are reduced by the teacher intervening and providing the correct answers ?

4 Open questions with terminal comments

Treatment D was the same treatment as Treatment F in all respects except that the discussion was cut short by the teacher providing the right answers to questions where the pupils were not able to after one or two attempts. Comparison of Treatments D and F in Figure 4 indicates that telling pupils the answers to questions they cannot answer has a detrimental effect on the level of achievement.

Summarizing these interpretations of the data, it seems that asking questions is a better procedure than not asking questions, but it does not seem to matter if the pupils actually participate in answering the questions. If the questions are not closely structured, telling pupils the answer is less effective than requiring them to answer for themselves, but the latter procedure will take considerably longer. When time taken is held constant, covering more content through the use of highly structured questions is more effective than using less highly structured questions and covering less content.

It seems evident that pupil achievement is a function both of the information conveyed by the discussion and the way in which that information is disclosed. Further detailed analysis of the effects of time taken by the lessons, the number of pupil responses, the effects of feedback from the teacher, and a number of other variables could be undertaken from the detailed records obtained from each of the lessons. These analyses are currently in the process of being completed. Already it is evident that these experimental studies have opened up many questions which require the designing of further experimental studies.

IV CONCLUDING NOTE

The experimental studies described in this article may be summarized in the following way. Our attention has been focused on a particular kind of teaching and on a particular kind of learning criterion. Within this area of interest, we have developed a descriptive category system and carried out some preliminary correlational studies. These correlational studies provided the ground work for a series of experiments which have generated a considerable body of detailed data about the relationships between selected teacher behaviours and measures of pupil learning. We hope that analysis of this body of data will provide the basis for the construction of a systematic psychological theory which accounts for the major dimensions of pupil learning in the classroom.

A preliminary description of an appropriate theory has already been prepared (Nuthall, 1971) but the data generated by the experimental studies has also suggested the need for further descriptive and correlational studies. It is evident that we must pay closer attention to the quality of pupil responses and find a system of describing the way teacher questions are directed to pupils of differing levels of ability. It is also evident that greater attention needs to be paid to the informational content and quality of the teacher's verbal communications. To this end, we are currently engaged in a correlational study in which pupil achievement is related to measures of the syntactical and semantic characteristics of the teacher's language.

Perhaps the best way to represent the studies reported in this article is to claim that we have attempted to reverse the usual role of theory in pedagogical research. Frequently experimental studies are carried out to 'prove' *a priori* claims about what teaching should be like. Generally such claims are simplistic and are derived from theoretical positions which are borrowed from other areas of research and misrepresent the complex realities of the classroom situation (Nuthall and Snook, in press). The studies reported in this article represent a conscious attempt to create experimental methods which are maximally responsive to the full complexities of the classroom situation.

If the research seems to be narrowly conceived, it is not because we are committed to the view that the variables we have studied are more important than any others. It is because we have had to begin our exploration of a complex situation at a point where some kind of success seemed probable. We can lay claim to having discovered some reliable information about the relationships that exist between teacher behaviours and pupil learning. Such information is rare.

BIBLIOGRAPHY

FLANDERS, N. A. (1960). *Teacher Influence, Pupil Attitudes and Achievement.* Final Report, Co-operative Research Project No. 397, US Office of Education. University of Minnesota.

FRANCIS, K. A. E. (1971). 'A study of the effect of teacher intention and class level on teaching behaviour and pupil thinking and learning in the classroom'. Unpublished Masters thesis. University of Canterbury.

HUGHES, D. (1971). 'An experimental investigation of the effects of certain teacher behaviours on pupil achievement'. Paper presented at the New Zealand Psychological Society Conference, Christchurch, N.Z.

JAYNE, C. D. (1945). 'A study of the relationship between teaching procedures and educational outcomes', *J. Exper. Educ.*, 14, 101–34.

LORD, F. M. (1969). 'Statistical adjustments when comparing pre-existing groups', *Psy. Bull.*, 72, 336–7.

NUTHALL, G. A. (1971). 'A theory of classroom learning'. Paper presented at the 43rd Conference of the Australian and New Zealand Association for the Advancement of Science, Brisbane.

NUTHALL, G. A. et al. (1970). *System for Analysis of Verbal Interaction in Class Lessons.* Mimeograph. Christchurch, NZ: University of Canterbury Teaching Research Project.

NUTHALL, G. A. and LAWRENCE, P. J. (1965). *Thinking in the Classroom.* Wellington, NZ: New Zealand Council for Educational Research.

NUTHALL, G. A. and SNOOK, I. A. 'Contemporary Models of Teaching'. In: TRAVERS, R. M. W. (Ed.) *The Second Handbook of Research on Teaching.* Chicago: Rand McNally. (In press.)

SIMON, A. and BOYER, E. G. (Eds.) (1968). *Mirrors for Behaviour: An Anthology of Classroom Observation Instruments.* Philadelphia: Research for Better Schools, Inc.

SMITH, B. OTHANEL. (1961). 'A concept of teaching'. In: SMITH, B. OTHANEL and ENNIS, R. H. (Eds.) *Language and Concepts in Education.* Chicago: Rand McNally.

THORNDIKE, E. L. (1906). *The Principles of Teaching Based on Psychology.* New York: A. G. Seiler.

WATSON, J. B. (1913). 'Psychology as the behaviourist views it', *Psychol. Rev.*, 20, 158–77.

Teachers' Assessments of their Pupils

M. Cameron-Jones and A. Morrison
University of Dundee

Assessment study covers a large field. In educational research such different topics as test construction, test use and marking, and the social skills involved in 'knowing' another person may be placed within it. It may investigate time units as long as a formal terminal examination and as short as a single teacher-pupil interchange. And it has to do not only with the written material which is so frequently the concern of formal testing and examining, but also with oral, facial, gestural and other kinds of behaviour. What all of these apparent diversities have in common is some connection with the process of attending to and interpreting information.

When one moves into any field for study, it is useful to make explicit one's descriptive framework, to make clear one's point of view. The most generalizable framework within which to fit one's thoughts about assessment is TOTE (Miller *et al*, 1960), a feedback loop. TOTE is a way of describing the kinds of acts which are worked through during the performance of any task. These acts are first T, a test for discrepancies between the present situation and the desired situation: secondly there is O, a stage of operation, when some action is performed to reduce the gap between what is the case and what is desired: this is followed by a further test for discrepancy. Testing and operating acts continue until E, the exit stage, when, the goal reached, the task is completed. TOTE is a general description of any kind of goal-directed behaviour and can be used to make clear what is involved in performing any single task or series of tasks. Hence it is applicable to the activities of teachers. Teachers are assumed to have goals, and these goals (pupil guidance and counselling, course-organization and, of course, teaching itself) can be viewed as a complex series of operations performed in the light of the information obtained by testing.

If one takes this view, one must assume that testing acts are central within teaching. Further, one would assume the desirability of accurate testing acts, since teaching, by this model, does not just include, but is, some series of diverse operating acts each of which will be more, or less, appropriate according to the accuracy of the antecedent test. Where test actions are sufficiently ill-performed, Hirst (1971) would refuse the label teaching to the operations following. He does, however, allow that '. . .we are inclined to think that there could be teaching even when the present state of the pupils is grossly misjudged.' TOTE and similar frameworks (Runkel, 1964) do incline one to think in this way, i.e. to view teaching as a stream of operating acts intended to reduce discrepancies between a pupil's (more *or less* accurately perceived) present state, and some desirable future state.

TOTE seems to be a useful general model for research on teachers. It can be elaborated for the specific purposes of assessment study. Thus for research on testing, it is useful to see T (the test action) as a two-phase one consisting in (i) selecting and (ii) interpreting information. One would then describe a teacher's formal testing in terms of (i) giving out work and (ii) marking it, and her assessment behaviour during teaching sequences as (i) soliciting responses from pupils and (ii) reacting to those responses. Since TOTE is an adaptable general model, it permits a 'multi-measure' study (Campbell, 1957), and so, within its framework, one can examine both cognitive and affective judgment. And one can study both assessment-accuracy and assessment-process—two aspects of assessment said (Warr and Knapper, 1968) to have often been divorced in empirical research.

The design of this study

No experiments were carried out during this work, since the research was to be a 'naturalistic' (Willems and Raish, 1969) study of assessment in the 'everyday life' setting of the school (McHenry, 1971).

Sample. There were 17 teachers in the study (eight men and nine women) and each was the sole English teacher of a class and taught the class no other subject. Their classes were first-year mixed ability classes following the Common Course in six comprehensive schools in eastern Scotland.

Measures. At the beginning and the end of the school year the classes completed the Bristol Achievement English Language Test (Brimer, 1969) and scales to measure their attitudes to school, to English and to English lessons. The pupils also provided autobiographical information.

The pupils' responses were used to measure the accuracy of their teachers' assessments. For their cognitive assessments, the teachers were asked to rank their pupils on the Bristol Test, to estimate the comparative difficulty for the class of the sub-tests, and to compare the class's general performance on the test with the performance of the other classes in the sample. For their affective assessments, the teachers were asked to predict pupil's responses to the attitude scales. Further, the teachers were asked to give biographical reports about pupils.

To describe the process of assessment in the classroom, an observation schedule was used to analyse the tape-recorded lessons taught by the teachers.

The measures used in the study are described in the appendix. They yielded data on various facets of teachers' assessments, and these are the data discussed in this paper.

I THE CLASSROOM OBSERVATIONS

In ordinary language, and for philosophers of language, the paradigm assessment act is the making of a rating. Thus Searle (1969): 'Giving an assessment will characteristically involve (among other things), assigning a grading label; and, conversely, assigning one of them will characteristically be giving an assessment, evaluation, or the like. And the term assigned will indicate the kind of assessment made—favourable or unfavourable, high or low, and so on.'

Assessment study is concerned, however, not only with how teachers rate or react to their pupils' responses but also with the ways in which teachers press for or solicit those responses. Its dual interest is reflected for example in its study of examination questions as well as the marking of examination answers. The observation schedule described here was developed as a way of describing classroom assessment in the process of occurring. It categorizes the components of the two aspects of the assessment process and orders the various categories into two major classes called solicitations and reactions. Solicitations are information-seeking acts: they are those teacher behaviours which press for a response from a pupil, for example 'Sit up straight now', 'What is this story about?' Reactions, on the other hand, offer various kinds of judgments on pupil behaviour, for example, 'Very good', 'Your vocabulary seems to have shrunk all of a sudden'.

It seems sure that few philosophers of language would readily discuss questioning, or other modes of solicitation, under the heading of assessment, and yet the propriety of searching teacher discourse for assessment acts was suggested by a philosopher's (Austin, 1962) recognition of performatives: 'The name performative indicates that the issuing of the utterance is the performing of an action—it is not normally thought of as just saying something'. This taken, one may claim to be describing what it is that teachers do in saying what they say. As, under normal conditions, saying 'Hello' is greeting, so saying 'Tell me'

Table 1: *Categories of solicitation identified by the schedule*

S1	Management.
S2	Social.
S3	Procedural requests/queries.
S4	Naming/calling upon.
S5	Tests for congruence (1).
S6	Tests for congruence (2). Rhetorical questions.
S7	Second-order questions.
S8	Knowledge.
S9	Comprehension.
S10	Application.
S11	Analysis.
S12	Synthesis.
S13	Evaluation.
S14	Receiving.
S15	Responding.
S16	Valuing.
S17	Commitment.
S18	Organization.
*S19	Characterization.
S20	Secondary solicitation (completion) cognitive.
S21	Secondary solicitation (completion) affective.
S22	Secondary solicitation (refinement) cognitive.
S23	Secondary solicitation (refinement) affective.
S24	Secondary solicitation (correction) cognitive.
S25	Secondary solicitation (correction) affective.
S26	Provision.
S27	Services.
S28	Referral—assignment.
S29	Cognitive, without clues.
S30	Affective, without clues.
S31	Open solicitations.

*An empty category throughout pilot studies and research.

Table 2: *Categories of reaction identified by the schedule*

R1	Knowledge
R2	Comprehension
R3	Application
R4	Analysis
R5	Synthesis
R6	Evaluation
R7	Receiving
R8	Responding
R9	Valuing
R10	Commitment
R11	Organization
*R12	Characterization
R13	Scanning
R14	Acknowledging
R15	Simple Praise
R16	Simple Reproof
R17	Elaborate Praise
R18	Elaborate Reproof
R19	Simple Confirmation
R20	Simple Denial
R21	Repeating pupil response positively
R22	Repeating pupil response negatively
R23	Positive restatement of pupil response
R24	Negative restatement of pupil response
R25	Elaborate confirmation
R26	Elaborate denial
R27	Positive management
R28	Negative management
R29	Historical management-related, positive
R30	Historical management-related, negative
R31	Historical achievement-related, positive
R32	Historical achievement-related, negative
R33	Positive role ratings
R34	Negative role ratings
R35	Social
R36	Teacher's self-assessments, positive
R37	Teacher's self-assessments, negative

*An empty category throughout pilot studies and research

is soliciting and saying 'That's a good answer' is reacting. Searle (1969) formulates the procedure neatly as 'X counts as Y in context C', and by this formula it makes no sense to ask 'How do you know that saying "Who was George Washington?" is soliciting?', since in short, one identifies the acts by appealing to convention. In other terms, then, by adopting this conceptual posture one is declaring one's interest in what Biddle (1967) calls the 'objective characteristics' of a teacher's talk. Such characteristics include non-verbal force indicators, so when 'You've made a really marvellous job of it' is said in certain tones (for example of sarcasm or contempt), this is coded as a reproof.

The observation schedule, ordered in two classes (of solicitation and reaction) which accord with an elaborated TOTE, allows one to map the business of assessment in the classroom in terms of the frequency of occurrence of those assessment acts identified by the schedule. The schedule identifies 68 kinds of assessment act. These acts are listed here and followed by examples of each.

Some examples of category-members

Solicitations

S1   Management solicitations. 'Now I want you to be really quiet.'

S2   Social solicitations. 'You keep pigeons, don't you ?'; 'And how's the leg today, then ?' These relate to health, family and other out-of-school affairs.

S3   Procedural requests/queries. 'Did I give them out ?'; 'Tell me if you need a book'; 'Remember to pass these in at the end'.

S4   Naming/calling upon. 'Sarah ?'; 'Anyone ?'; 'Boys ?' These follow the throwing of a question to the class, and specify the respondent.

S5   Tests for congruence. 'Okay ?'; 'Surely ?'; 'Right ?'

S6   Tests for congruence. Rhetorical questions.

S7   Second-order questions. 'Are you sure you know ?'; 'Do you really understand ?'

S8 to S13 are defined by reference to Bloom (1965).

S8   Knowledge. 'What was the date of this ?'

S9   Comprehension. 'Is there a general theme in all of this ?'

S10   Application. ('Yes. Texas for one. . . And in some parts of the East. . .) So now there's North Sea oil, what can we expect for Aberdeen ?'

S11   Analysis. ('When you look, he's put something in here which goes against his own argument.) Which part is it ?'

S12   Synthesis. ('Lots of things get tipped up there but I want to think about plastic bottles for just now.) What could we do with them which would actually make them an asset to Dundee ?'

S13   Evaluation. ['It (Genesis) does put it differently in relation to Adam and Eve . . . different from your Science books. Or History books for that matter. But we don't just have to toss a coin or something and choose one to be right. We can sort out the problem.] How ?'

S14 to S19 are defined by reference to Krathwohl (1969) though with S14 extending to his 2.1 level.

S14   Receiving. 'Do you hear a quicker rhythm now ?'

S15   Responding. 'Would you like to do some more ?'; 'Did you find that a bit long ?'

S16   Valuing. 'Did you use your own money ?' (To buy Puffin edition of class novel.)

S17   Commitment. 'Have you done this every day ?' (Pupil has kept up a five-year poetry diary for three years to date.)

S18   Organization. ('Obeying the law . . . obeying orders. It's not at all obvious what you should do. Last week . . .) Why was it the right thing to do from your point of view ?' (To defend a friend against bullies, though the pupil's parents had forbidden the friendship.)

S19   Characterization. An empty category, i.e. no instances were found of this either during the pilot studies or during this particular study. Of this category the taxonomists state, 'Realistically, formal education generally cannot reach this level, at least in our society'. (Krathwohl, 1969.)

S20 and S21. Secondary solicitation (completion). Whether cognitive or affective, identified by context. 'And ?. . .'; 'And *also*. . .; 'Go on'; 'Anything else ?. . .'; 'And *another* point ?. . .'

S22 and S23. Secondary solicitation (refinement). Whether cognitive or affective, identified by context. 'Develop that a bit for me'; 'Tell me that again but in a better way'; '(That's a very vague sort of answer though.) Do better than that'; '(Yes.) So what *is* your argument then ?'; '(Yes. Conditions.) What *sort* of conditions ?'; '(Yes. It would affect you.) *How* would it affect you ?'

S24 and S25. Secondary solicitation (correction). Whether cognitive or affective, identified by context. 'Can you put yourself right ?'; 'But what did you say just then that couldn't possibly be right ?'; 'But, from what you're saying, it is likely a feeling of real *fear* you're getting with it ?'

S26   Provision. Teacher provides an aid (e.g. pencil, extra book) to a pupil. A silent category.

S27   Services. Teacher performs a task for a pupil, e.g. finds the place in a book. A silent category. (No instances in this particular study.)

S28   Referral-assignment. 'Write it down'; 'Read that bit to me'; 'Look for page 72.'

S29 and S30   Solicitations without clues, discriminable by context as cognitive or affective. 'Well ?'; 'What can we say about this ?'; 'Tell me about this.'

S31   Open solicitations. Take forms similar to S29 and S30, but are not discriminable as cognitive or affective.

Reactions

R1 to R12. These are modifying reactions, grouped in levels corresponding to S8 to S19. Modifiers are conjoined to a pupil response, either by explicit reference or by grammatical conjunction. When conjunction ceases, coding ceases, an Operation being then supposed to have begun. Examples are:

Pupil	'When you're not well.'
Teacher	'(When you're not well), as a rule.'
Teacher	'(How did the baby react ?)'
Pupil	'He cooed and laughed.'
Teacher	'When the boy came in. (Yes.) Because he hadn't seen him for a long time.'
Pupil	'Part of everyday life.'
Teacher	'(Not part of everyday life), unless he was an undertaker of course.'
Pupil	'The Welfare State.'
Teacher	'(The Welfare State.) Which helps you if you are off sick or need the doctor.'
Pupil	'Tea was brought at five-o-clock.'
Teacher	'(Yes.) With some ceremony perhaps.'
Pupil	'In the fourth verse.'
Teacher	'(Yes), and actually in the last as well.'
Pupil	'They are going to swop places.'
Teacher	'(Yes), at least he's going to become the road man.'
Pupil	'They could all be a wee bit right.'
Teacher	'(Yes) but we've all got to sort out some time what we really believe in and what we really ought to do.'
Teacher	'(Yes) and to go on from what you've said . . .'
Teacher	'(Not really) because, as you almost got round to saying . . .'
Teacher	'. . .and, from what John's just said. . .'

R13   Scanning. Teacher scans pupil work. A silent category. One element less than or equal to five seconds.

R14   Acknowledging. Reactions in which positive/negative discriminations were not possible. 'Mmm'; other non-verbal noises; 'I suppose.'

R15   Simple praise. 'Aha!'; 'Good'; 'Good boy!'

R16   Simple reproof. 'That's daft'; 'Stupid girl'; 'Again' (with contempt).

R17   Elaborate praise. 'You've thought that out very cunningly!'; 'That's a nice concise statement of it you've made'; 'You've put an excellent case for it.'

R18   Elaborate reproof. 'Of course, that's just the first thing that came into your head'; 'You're just not careful enough in your statements'; 'You've contradicted yourself all over the place.'

R19   Simple confirmation. 'Yes'; 'Quite'; 'That's right.'

R20   Simple denial. 'No'; 'That's wrong'; 'Not that'; 'Not it'.

R21 and R22   Repeating pupil response. Positive or negative according to vocal and contextual clues.

R23 and R24   Restatements of pupil response. These are lexical or structural transformations, judged positive or negative by vocal and contextural clues.

Pupil   'They're going away.'
Teacher   '(Yes) they're emigrating.'

Pupil   'It's to do with diet.'
Teacher   '(No.) It's not related to nutrition.'

R25   Elaborate confirmation. '. . .and you're quite right to think it's that'; 'It's absolutely as you say.'

R26   Elaborate denial. 'The wrong bit of it seems to have got over to you'; (No.) That's not the proper term for it.'

R27   Positive management-related reactions. 'That's something very nice to see.' (To silent seated pupils.) No instances in this particular study.

R28   Negative management-related reactions. 'The whole school will hear you yelling'; 'You're making too much noise.'

R29   Historical management-related reactions, positive. 'You've always been a pleasant class.' No instances in this particular study.

R30   Historical management-related reactions, negative. 'I've had opposition from this corner all this year.'

R31   Historical achievement-related reactions, positive. 'You lot were always quick at that.'

R32   Historical achievement-related reactions, negative. 'You seem to have been getting worse at this since Christmas.'

R33   Positive role ratings. '. . .the only one who's paying attention.'
R34   Negative role ratings. 'What a lazy lot you are today':

Teacher   'What's the cat doing?'
Pupil   'Going to sleep'.
Teacher   '(Going to sleep.) Like some of you.'

R35 Social responding. These relate to health, family and other topic-irrelevant, out-of-school affairs. 'That's nice'; 'Did you really!'; "No!'

Teacher '(You're the last of the Ritchies, aren't you?)'
Pupil 'Yes.'
Teacher 'Aye. I've taught all of the Ritchies by now!'

R36 Teacher's self-assessments, positive. 'I got it joined just right.' No instances in this study.

R37 Teacher's self-assessments, negative. 'I read that very badly'; '(I can't remember myself now why I wrote that up.) It's wrong, anyway.'

Findings

The schedule was used to analyse the assessment behaviour of the 17 teachers in the sample. Their periods of teaching were tape-recorded and analysed afterwards. The observation visits took place in the spring term, each at a normally timetabled period, the teachers having been asked not to set silent written work for the whole of the period, but to include some oral work. The teachers were given the impression that their pupils were the observation-interest, the tape-recorder being necessary to 'record the kinds of contributions made'. Some teachers taught a double period, and others taught two single related periods. Certain parts of the observed periods were not analysed (for example, when the teacher was called away from the room, or times when the pupils wrote silently and the teacher was occupied at her desk). The average period actually coded was 57 minutes and the average number of pupils present was 30. Though the teachers and pupils reported at the time that the lessons had gone as they normally did, one teacher did write, some months afterwards, to say that the presence of an observer must necessarily affect transactions in a classroom.

Detailed observational data raise problems of presentation. Mean scores, as used by Duthie (1970) are also presented here, the scores being first converted to a 60-minute base. The findings on both classes of assessment act are clearly comparable with those reported for four teachers randomly selected from those observed during the development of the schedule (Cameron-Jones, 1972).

Solicitations

Table 3 gives mean solicitation frequencies.

This table has some value as a descriptive record. It shows that certain kinds of solicitation occur comparatively frequently in classrooms and that other kinds are very much less common. It also shows that teachers vary considerably in their solicitation patterns, since the standard deviations for some categories are bigger than the means. Beyond this, however, it is difficult to think in an organized way about a list of data like this one, and to obtain understandable and economical descriptions it is necessary to conflate[1] the categories in various ways. When conflations were performed upon the data from each teacher, frequencies from the silent categories (S26, S27) were dropped from the analysis, the conflation-yield to refer only to each teacher's oral solicitations.

[1]Convention dictates modes of category-conflation, conflation being performed to reduce the data. For example, R15 to R26 are all topic-relevant rating reactions, i.e. ratings which relate to the manifest topic of the lesson (rather than, for example, to procedural or management affairs). Of these R15, 17, 19, 21, 23 and 25 are conflated to express the positive or favourable reactions in the set. These reactions are positive or favourable by conventional definition. One may rate something favourably or unfavourably, but one cannot praise it unfavourably.

Table 3: *Mean solicitation frequencies*

		Mean	SD
S1	Management	4·30	5·34
S2	Social	4·63	8·21
S3	Procedural requests/queries	16·08	7·66
S4	Naming/calling upon	59·80	32·15
S5	Tests for congruence (1)	6·16	5·54
S6	Tests for congruence (2), Rhetorical questions	2·44	3·16
S7	Second-order questions	4·11	4·35
S8	Knowledge	22·46	18·23
S9	Comprehension	31·48	22·83
S10	Application	3·15	4·98
S11	Analysis	5·33	5·78
S12	Synthesis	2·46	3·84
S13	Evaluation	1·99	4·28
S14	Receiving	5·61	10·23
S15	Responding	34·14	18·97
S16	Valuing	9·26	13·77
S17	Commitment	2·69	6·02
S18	Organization	0·54	2·22
S19	Characterization	—	—
S20	Secondary solicitation (completion), cognitive	14·59	14·90
S21	Secondary solicitation (completion), affective	5·84	8·35
S22	Secondary solicitation (refinement), cognitive	11·02	11·09
S23	Secondary solicitation (refinement), affective	8·02	8·01
S24	Secondary solicitation (correction), cognitive	3·23	4·01
S25	Secondary solicitation (correction), affective	1·20	2·80
S26	Provision	0·59	1·30
S27	Services	—	—
S28	Referral—assignment	20·81	14·35
S29	Cognitive, without clues	0·32	0·96
S30	Affective, without clues	0·84	1·73
S31	Open solicitations	3·26	6·08

(1) Solicitations categorized within the taxonomists' classificatory schemes were, as before, located at the simplest levels (Tables 4 to 7), though the English teachers did test more frequently at Bloom's level of comprehension, than had the teachers described in the previous paper (Cameron-Jones, 1972).

Table 4: *Cognitive taxonomized solicitations (percentages)*

		Mean	SD
S8	Knowledge	32·55	20·88
S9	Comprehension	47·00	27·12
S10	Application	4·61	8·39
S11	Analysis	8·10	8·41
S12	Synthesis	3·83	4·89
S13	Evaluation	3·92	7·39

Table 5: *Cognitive taxonomized solicitations. Hierarchical groupings (percentages)*

	Mean	SD
Simple Pair (S8, 9)	79·55	17·00
Middle Pair (S10, 11)	12·71	10·17
Complex Pair (S12, 13)	7·75	10·39

Table 6: *Affective taxonomized solicitations (percentages)*

		Mean	SD
S14	Receiving	12·81	21·23
S15	Responding	65·41	27·20
S16	Valuing	12·43	16·41
S17	Commitment	3·68	9·41
S18	Organization	0·38	1·57
S19	Characterization	—	—

Table 7: *Affective taxonomized solicitations. Hierarchical groupings (percentages)*

	Mean	SD
Simple Pair (S14, 15)	85·52	20·51
Middle Pair (S16, 17)	16·10	19·88
Complex Pair (S18, 19)	0·38	1·57

(2) When Probing Questions (S20 to 25) were expressed as a percentage of Instructional-interactional solicitations (S5 to 31, excluding 26, 27 and 28) their proportion was 21·07 (Table 8).

Table 8: *Probing questions as a percentage of instructional-interactional solicitations*

	Mean	SD
Probing Questions	21·07	10·25

(3) Solicitations with clues (S1 to 28) formed by far the larger proportion of all solicitations (Table 9).

Table 9: *All solicitations (percentages)*

	Mean	SD
With clues	98·65	2·06
Without clues	1·35	2·06

(4) Other groupings (Table 10) revealed the dominance of topic-relevant and procedural solicitations, and the small amount of social solicitation.

Table 10: *All solicitations (percentages)*

	Mean	SD
Topic-relevant (S8 to 31)	65·60	6·65
Procedural (S3, 4)	26·52	6·03
Pedagogic (S5–7)	4·55	2·51
Social (S2)	1·49	2·32
Management (S1)	1·85	2·28

(5) Conflations of cognitive and affective categories (among S8 to 25, and 29, 30) revealed the salience of cognition as the domain of soliciting concern (Table 11).

Table 11: *Domain of concern (percentages)*

	Mean	SD
Cognition	59·58	18·98
Affect	40·42	18·98

Reactions

Table 12 gives the array of mean reaction frequencies. For conflation, the silent category (R13) and the teachers' self-assessments (R36 and 37) were dropped from the analysis, the conflations to be only of each teacher's oral reactions to his pupils.

Table 12: *Mean reaction frequencies*

		Mean	SD
R1	Knowledge	20·82	17·86
R2	Comprehension	12·13	10·04
R3	Application	2·26	4·14
R4	Analysis	1·50	2·18
R5	Synthesis	0·67	1·82
R6	Evaluation	1·17	2·44
R7	Receiving	0·78	1·60
R8	Responding	8·76	8·26
R9	Valuing	3·37	5·30
R10	Commitment	0·62	1·40
R11	Organization	0·12	0·49
R12	Characterization	—	—
R13	Scanning	3·95	8·39
R14	Acknowledging	25·71	15·51
R15	Simple Praise	6·23	6·81
R16	Simple Reproof	0·56	1·15
R17	Elaborate Praise	4·65	5·74
R18	Elaborate Reproof	2·61	1·89
R19	Simple Confirmation	56·90	34·63
R20	Simple Denial	8·70	8·12
R21	Repeating pupil response positively	36·86	16·75
R22	Repeating pupil response negatively	2·14	2·59
R23	Positive restatement of pupil response	21·36	13·56
R24	Negative restatement of pupil response	0·99	1·25
R25	Elaborate confirmation	12·17	6·74
R26	Elaborate denial	9·26	8·50
R27	Positive management	—	—
R28	Negative management	9·99	11·39
R29	Historical management-related, positive	—	—
R30	Historical management-related, negative	0·06	0·26
R31	Historical achievement-related, positive	1·20	2·10
R32	Historical achievement-related, negative	1·11	1·69
R33	Positive role ratings	1·11	1·71
R34	Negative role ratings	10·51	5·86
R35	Social	4·30	8·90
R36	Teacher's self-assessments, positive	—	—
R37	Teacher's self-assessments, negative	0·27	0·76

(1) As before, regulative reactions were predominantly negative (Table 13) but ratings of responses which referred to the content of the lesson were more often positive (Table 14). The latter tended more often to be simple than elaborate (Table 15).

Table 13: *Regulative reactions (percentages)*

	Mean	SD
Negative (R28, 30, 34)	92·59	19·26
Positive (R27, 29, 33)	7·41	19·26

Table 14: *Topic-relevant rating reactions (R15 to R26)*
        (percentages)

	Mean	SD
Positive	85·44	8·02
Negative	14·62	7·96

Table 15: *Topic-relevant rating reactions (percentages)*

	Mean	SD
Simple (R15, 16, 19, 20, 21, 22)	67·67	8·81
Elaborate (R17, 18, 23, 24, 25, 26)	32·33	8·81

(2) Again, modifying reactions were located most frequently at the simple cognitive or simple affective levels (Tables 16 to 19).

Table 16: *Cognitive modifying reactions (percentages)*

		Mean	SD
R1	Knowledge	50·75	26·02
R2	Comprehension	33·75	21 63
R3	Application	5·40	9·26
R4	Analysis	4·50	6·74
R5	Synthesis	1·80	3·76
R6	Evaluation	3·79	6·74

Table 17: *Cognitive modifying reactions. Hierarchical groupings (percentages)*

	Mean	SD
Simple Pair (R1, 2)	84·50	13·62
Middle Pair (R3, 4)	9·91	10·68
Complex Pair (R5, 6)	5·60	8·93

Table 18: *Affective modifying reactions (percentages)*

		Mean	SD
R7	Receiving	5·50	14·89
R8	Responding	64·93	34·86
R9	Valuing	15·01	21·24
R10	Commitment	2·51	6·51
R11	Organization	0·30	1·22
R12	Characterization	—	—

Table 19: *Affective modifying reactions. Hierarchical groupings (percentages)*

	Mean	SD
Simple Pair (R7, 8)	70·42	35·76
Middle Pair (R9, 10)	17·52	24·54
Complex Pair (R11, 12)	0·30	1·22

(3) Groupings made of each teacher's total reaction emission revealed the predominance of critical ratings and of modifying reactions (Table 20).

Table 20: *All reactions (percentages)*

	Mean	SD
Critical ratings (R19–26)	54·21	10·77
Modifying reactions (R1–12)	19·12	6·90
Evaluative ratings (R15–18)	5·19	3·33
Acknowledging (R14)	9·80	5·65
Management ratings (R27, 28)	4·33	4·84
Historical management ratings (R29, 30)	0·03	0·14
Historical achievement ratings (R31, 32)	0·98	1·23
Role ratings (R33, 34)	4·84	3·15
Social responding (R35)	1·50	2·95

Again, reactions referred more often to the topic of the lesson than to regulative, procedural or social affairs (Table 21).

Table 21: *All reactions (percentages)*

	Mean	SD
Topic-relevant (R1–26)	88·44	9·06
Topic-irrelevant (R27–35)	11·56	9·06

(4) Finally, conflation within the modifiers (R1 to 12) revealed (Table 22) that cognition (which had also dominated solicitation) was the domain of major modifying action.

Table 22: *Domain of concern, modifying reactions (percentages)*

	Mean	SD
Cognition (R1–6)	76·05	19·19
Affect (R7–12)	23·95	19·19

Discussion

Compared with the previously reported data (Cameron-Jones, 1972) derived from the application of this schedule to periods of teaching of other subjects, the English teachers more often press for pupil-responses, and give modifying feedback, at Bloom's level of comprehension: they also tend more often to ambiguous feedback (R14) and less often to self-congratulation (R36). Perhaps this last is because teachers' demonstrative tasks in English are less hazardous than those (dissection, map drawing) performed by other teachers.

In featuring simple questioning (Hughes, 1965), and simple (Zahorik, 1968), positive (Bellack *et al.*, 1966; Meux and Smith, 1964) feedback of topic-relevant responses, the data are in accord with those of earlier researchers. Accepting the teachers' and pupils' reports of the normality of the observations, assessment in the first-year class is typically topic-centred (Tables 10 and 21), simple in demands (Tables 4, 5, 6, 7 and 8) and judgments (Tables 15, 16, 17, 18 and 19), clear and specific in requirements (Table 9) and falling commonly within the cognitive domain (Tables 11 and 22). Finally, academic judgments tend towards the positive (Table 14) while regulative judgments tend towards the negative (Table 13).

II   CROSS-CATEGORY EFFECTS IN TEACHERS' ASSESSMENTS

In giving simple descriptions of teachers' assessment behaviour, the preceding section is an example of a way in which observational data can be presented and be of interest in themselves. But such data can of course also be used as part of a larger study.

In this section of the paper various other analyses of the observations which were reported in the preceding section will be employed. They will give one method, along with others, of examining whether teachers have different ways of assessing different kinds of pupils. At various times during the academic year the teachers in the sample ranked their pupils for ability in English. The research interest lay in discovering whether these rankings were associated with consistent differences in the teachers' other assessments of the pupils. Thus this section reports some aspects of assessment-accuracy and assessment-process in teachers' perceptions of pupils ranked respectively as high and low in ability in English by their teachers.

The study of cross-category effects in teachers' assessments of their pupils is not new. Traditionally, this area has been researched by investigations of irrelevant noise in teachers' scholastic assessments (Briggs, 1970; Hadley, 1954; Huck and Bounds, 1972; Meltzer, 1971) or by factor-analytic work (Hallworth, 1964) on teachers' ratings of pupils' personality traits ('. . . the pupil with highest intelligence and attainment being attributed other desirable personality traits.') More recently, behaviour data have been gaining increasing currency in this field, and one concern has been to discover the co-variants of different teacher-behaviours towards different groups of pupils in their classrooms (Brophy and Good, 1970; Meichenbaum, Bowers and Ross, 1969; Silberman, 1969). Previous work on teacher-preferences (Davidson and Lang 1960; Feshbach, 1969; Morrison *et al.*, 1965) theories of instrumental relevance (Rommetveit, 1960) and of over-categorization (Allport, 1958), and one's own interpretations of teachers' staffroom talk, suggested that a teacher's perceptions of a child's ability in a subject would be associated with differences on other, dissimilar assessment-measures; specifically, it seemed probable that, of their high-ranked pupils, the teachers would:

(i) store more accurate biographical information. The teachers' scores on the Interpersonal Knowledge Schedules were the data used to test this.

(ii) feel more confident of their knowledge. The number of *attempted* answers the teachers made on the Interpersonal Knowledge Schedules were the data used to test this.

(iii) make more accurate predictions of attitudinal responses. Teachers' predictions of the pupils' responses on the three attitude scales were the data used to test this.

(iv) expect more positive expressions of attitude than in fact the pupils gave. (And, for their low-ranked pupils, expect more negative expressions of attitude than those pupils gave.) An analysis of the direction of error-choice[1] on the three attitude scales yielded the data to test this.

And also that, to their high-ranked pupils, teachers would in the classroom:

(v) send more neutral or favourable assessment messages, and

(vi) send fewer negative assessment messages.

To test hypotheses (v) and (vi) the observation data were used, all the pupils present being divided at the median and then treated as two groups.[2]

The foregoing were expressed as null hypotheses and tested.

Results

(i) An application of the Wilcoxon Matched-Pairs Signed-Ranks Test (Siegel, 1956) showed that teachers had given more accurate biographical information about their high-ranked pupils than their low ($p = \cdot005$) and that

(ii) the teachers had been more confident of their knowledge of their high-ranked pupils than their low ($p = \cdot005$), i.e. the teachers had made more attempts to give biographical information about their high-ranked pupils.

---

[1]'Error' for these analyses was defined as follows. The scales allowed for responses in the range VSA, SA, A, N, D, SD, VSD, with N locating the don't know or no opinion point. Only if teacher-prediction and pupil-response fell on opposite sides of N, was a teacher-error recorded. Positive error was recorded where the teacher's prediction for the pupil was in favour of the object (School, English, English lessons) and pupil-response was not: and negative error contrariwise. Where either party had chosen the N response, no error, of course, was recorded, so that an error was recorded and then scored for directionality (plus or minus) only where a teacher had made a clear prediction on an item on which the child had made an equally clear, but opposite, response.

[2]Target-records were made during the classroom observation periods by the observer with a seating plan, each target-child of an assessment being identified by his seat-number. Analyses were made only of individual pupil targets. Collective targets (whole class or group) were ignored for the study reported in this section. After the tape-recorded lesson, and on a separate sheet of paper, the teacher rank-ordered those pupils who were present, for 'general ability in English'. During post-session coding, each child continued to be identified by the number of his seat. But for the final protocols this label was translated into his teacher's rank for him. The rank-ordered class protocol was then divided at the median to yield the data for hypotheses (v) and (vi). (For all the measures used, to avoid observer-effects, and in accord with the demands of naturalistic studies, no rankings from any class were scored or analysed until the year's research was finished. Thus, teachers' rankings remained unknown to the observer until the final protocols were prepared at the end of the research.)

(iii) For neither their autumn nor their subsequent summer predictions on pupils' attitudes to school were the teachers' scores significantly different in accuracy. However, the autumn predictions on attitudes to English and to English lessons were significantly different in accuracy, in favour of the high-ranked pupils ($p = \cdot025$ and $\cdot01$, respectively), as were the subsequent summer predictions on those two scales ($p = \cdot025$ and $\cdot005$, respectively). Again the Wilcoxon Text was used.

(iv) Chi-squared analyses of the direction in which teachers had made their errors in prediction showed that, both in the autumn, and in the following summer, the teachers had, on all three scales, tended to make positive errors for their high-ranked pupils and negative errors for their low-ranked pupils, i.e. they had expected their high-ranked pupils to be more positive in attitude to school, to English and to English lessons than in fact they were, and their low-ranked pupils to be more negative in attitude to those three things than they were. These differences were significant at the $\cdot001$ level for all the tests performed.

(v) Wilcoxon Tests on the behaviour data showed that 'high' pupils had more often been the targets of certain neutral assessments in the classroom, i.e. there were significant differences in favour of high-ranking pupil-targets when the teachers were naming or calling upon a pupil in the classroom (e.g. 'Jane?', 'Morag?') and performing tests of congruence (e.g. 'Okay?', 'Agreed?'). On these two categories (S4 and S5) the differences in frequency were significant at the $\cdot005$ level. [Sarbin (1960) has listed some strategies of search used by assessors when seeking functionally relevant input. Soliciting he describes as selective probing, and adds that perhaps this strategy is applied when the assessor 'has a premise which he wants to confirm'.]

The Wilcoxon Tests showed, too, that high-ranked pupils had more often been the target of certain favourable assessment messages in the classroom, i.e. when teachers emitted simple confirmation (R19, significant at the $\cdot005$ level), and positive repetition of pupil response (R21, significant at the $\cdot01$ level), and positive restatement of pupil response (R23, significant at the $\cdot025$ level) and elaborate confirmation (R25, significant at the $\cdot005$ level).

(vi) The data on negative assessment messages did not attain statistical significance. In fact, though this was not significant, for *elaborate* denial (R26) the high-ranked pupils had more often been the targets.

Tables 23 and 24 show, however, that even where statistical significance was not attained, the data on many of the categories had fallen out in the predicted way. Low-ranked pupils had more often been the target of management solicitations (S1), of elaborate reproof (R18), of simple denial (R20), of negative repetition of pupil response (R22), of negative restatement of pupil response (R24), of negative management-related reactions (R28), and of negative role ratings (R34).

These observation data are derived from whole-class studies. Many more statistical significances have been reported from a study (Brophy and Good, 1970) which also used teachers' rankings prior to classroom observation, but in that work the researchers had selected from the rankings only six 'high' and six 'low' pupils for observation-study, and allow that 'by selecting subjects from the extremes of the distributions of teachers' rankings the chances of discovering differential teacher-treatment of the students were maximized.' For the Common Course Comprehensive School class, analyses which take account of every pupil present, seem, when statistically supported, of greater educational interest than partial analyses might be.

Table 23: *Table of more-frequent-target pupils for solicitation, and levels of* p

		p	More-frequent-target pupils
S1	Management	NS	Low
S2	Social	χ	High
S3	Procedural requests/queries	NS	High
S4	Naming/calling upon	·005	High
S5	Tests for congruence (1)	·005	High
S6	Tests for congruence (2), Rhetorical questions . . .	χ	High
S7	Second-order questions	NS	High
S8	Knowledge	NS	High
S9	Comprehension	NS	High
S10	Application	χ	Low
S11	Analysis	χ	High
S12	Synthesis	χ	Low
S13	Evaluation	χ	High
S14	Receiving	NS	Low
S15	Responding	NS	High
S16	Valuing	NS	Low
S17	Commitment	χ	High
S18	Organization	*	*
S19	Characterization	—	—
S20	Secondary solicitation (completion), cognitive . . .	NS	Low
S21	Secondary solicitation (completion), affective . . .	NS	Low
S22	Secondary solicitation (refinement), cognitive . . .	NS	High
S23	Secondary solicitation (refinement), affective . . .	NS	High
S24	Secondary solicitation (correction), cognitive . . .	NS	High
S25	Secondary solicitation (correction), affective . . .	χ	High
S26	Provision	χ	Low
S27	Services	—	—
S28	Referral—assignment	NS	High
S29	Cognitive, without clues	χ	Low
S30	Affective, without clues	*	*
S31	Open solicitations	χ	High

— (No observations)
χ (N less than 6)
* (Too few observations to test)

Discussion

As predicted, there are within these findings consistencies which are as much to be explained, perhaps, by the information-processing habits of the teachers as by the veridical characteristics of the children. For in sum the teachers know better and feel that they know better, those pupils they have ranked as high in ability in English. They can give more accurate biographical reports of them and can more accurately predict their attitudes to English and to what happens during English lessons. Further when the teachers do make errors in predicting the attitudes of their high-ranked pupils, these errors tend to be in the favourable direction: and also, there are some qualitative differences in teachers' behaviour towards the two groups of pupils.

Such findings as these about assessment-accuracy [hypotheses (i) and (iii)] are of some interest since there is theoretical (Miller *et al.*, 1960, Runkel, 1964) and empirical (Ojemann and Wilkinson, 1939; Penfold and Meldon, 1969) work which suggests the relevance of assessment-accuracy to teaching. But the findings about assessment-process are as much to be considered. Analyses of teacher confidence and of directionality of error [hypotheses (ii) and (iv)], for example, seem to show that teachers view their high and low-ranked pupils through different kinds of lenses. And the observation data tease out two different classroom worlds. For pupils in a class which has a 'Common' English course, it seems there are facets of the course which differ.

Table 24: *Table of more-frequent-target pupils for reaction, and levels of* p

		p	More-frequent-target pupils
R1	Knowledge	NS	Low
R2	Comprehension	NS	Low
R3	Application	χ	High
R4	Analysis	NS	High
R5	Synthesis	χ	High
R6	Evaluation	χ	Low
R7	Receiving	—	—
R8	Responding	NS	High
R9	Valuing	χ	High
R10	Commitment	χ	High
R11	Organization	*	*
R12	Characterization	—	—
R13	Scanning	χ	High
R14	Acknowledging	NS	Low
R15	Simple praise	NS	High
R16	Simple reproof	χ	High
R17	Elaborate praise	NS	High
R18	Elaborate reproof	NS	Low
R19	Simple confirmation	·005	High
R20	Simple denial	NS	Low
R21	Repeating pupil response positively	·01	High
R22	Repeating pupil response negatively	NS	Low
R23	Positive restatement of pupil respónse	·025	High
R24	Negative restatement of pupil response	NS	Low
R25	Elaborate confirmation	·005	High
R26	Elaborate denial	NS	High
R27	Positive management	—	—
R28	Negative management	NS	Low
R29	Historical management-related, positive	—	—
R30	Historical management-related, negative	*	*
R31	Historical achievement-related, positive	*	*
R32	Historical achievement-related, negative	*	*
R33	Positive role ratings	NS	High
R34	Negative role ratings	NS	Low
R35	Social	χ	High
R36	Teacher's self-assessments, positive	—	—
R37	Teacher's self-assessments, negative	*	*

— (No observations)
χ (N less than 6)
* (Too few observations to test)

III THE PROCESS-PRODUCT STUDY by A. Morrison

When researchers have examined the training of teachers in assessment-competence (Cortis and Dean, 1969, 1972; Goslin, 1967) or have investigated the assessments made by practising teachers (Carter, 1952; Eggleston and Kelly, 1969; Eggleston and Kerr, 1969), their interest has commonly been in formal, scholastic or clerical concerns. Studies of assessment as a social skill in teachers are comparatively rare (Penfold and Meldon, 1969) and those studies which define assessment both in social-psychological and in scholastic terms are very rare indeed. One such, directed by Nathaniel Gage (1955), did demand these two kinds of assessment-accuracy tasks from the teachers, but it did not study assessment-accuracy over an extended period of time. Nor did it obtain observational data of classroom assessment in the process of occurring.

The research reported in this section was designed as a 'process-product' study (Rosenshine and Furst, 1971). For the pupil variables, the measures of achievement and attitude were taken at the beginning and the end of the school year[1], and the school class was the statistical unit used: 'The class rather than the number of students appears to be the appropriate unit for research of this type because the investigator wishes to generalize to the behaviours of teachers' (Rosenshine, 1971).

The teacher variables in the study were their scores on the various assessment tasks. These tasks gave measures of the teachers' cognitive and affective assessment-accuracy, and a measure of the accuracy of their biographical knowledge of the pupils. The teacher-behaviour variables were given by the various scores the teachers obtained when the observation schedule was used to analyse the tape-recordings made of them at work with their classes. The tape-recorded behaviour data were treated as a single sample of verbal behaviour. That is, except in one instance[2] no analyses by pupil-target were included. Silent categories and the teachers' self-assessments were also excluded because the teachers' oral assessments of their pupils were the interest.

Before the process-product search began, there was a scrutiny by rank-order correlation coefficients among the pupils' scores alone. This search revealed that teachers' assessment skills may be less significant for their classes' achievements than they are for attitudes, since the scrutiny of the classes' summer achievement scores showed their most powerful associates to be the preceding autumn achievement scores. Whether the summer scores were expressed as medians or as means, of raw or of standardized scores, their two most powerful associates were the autumn mean raw and mean standardized scores. The strongest associates of the classes' summer scores on attitudes, however, were their teachers' assessment behaviours, which suggests that teachers work with more freedom within the area of pupil attitude than they do within the area of achievement.

It remained to be discovered which, of the testing acts researched, were the most significant facets of assessment so far as pupil outcome was concerned. A two-stage search strategy was employed to study this.

[1]For the sample of children taken as a whole, the standardized achievement scores differed little from occasion to occasion. (The difference between the autumn and the summer scores was −0·30.) However, there were slight negative shifts in mean attitude to school ($\bar{x} = -4\cdot34$, 17-item scale) to English ($\bar{x} = -2\cdot96$, 15-item scale) and to English lessons ($\bar{x} = -7\cdot14$, 17-item scale). Flanders (1968) reports similarly for his study of changes in pupil attitudes during the school year.

[2]Target-records were used to express each teacher's vicariously-taught pupils as a percentage of pupils present. A vicariously-taught pupil was one who was not the individual target of a soliciting or reacting act of any kind.

(a) **The first stage of search**

In the first process-product search, Spearman's correlations were performed to reduce the data to be submitted to the second-stage analysis.

In the final analysis the criterion pupil-outcome measures[1] were to be the mean and median shifts on the three attitude scales, and the mean and median shift in standardized achievement score, each pupil acting as his own control and so contributing to the whole-class score which was used as the statistical unit.

For this first-stage search, however, these measures were supplemented by various other ways of expressing the chosen outcomes, i.e. by mean and median raw achievement score shift (each pupil as his own control): and by shift on achievement (raw and standardized scores), and on attitude, using whole-class difference scores expressed as medians and as means.

(b) **The second stage of search**

The chosen level of correlation was ·425 ($p = < ·05$), and any teacher measure associated at this level or above with any pupil outcome measure, was viewed as a candidate for further study and retained for use in the second stage of search which in the event contained 46 teacher variables and the criterion pupil variables shown in Table 25.

Table 25: *Criterion pupil outcome measures*
(Class scores. Mean and median shift)

---

1. Attitudes to school.
2. Attitudes to English.
3. Attitudes to English Lessons.
4. English Language Achievement.
   Standardized scores.

Assessment-process. The teacher behaviour variables used to describe assessment-process were of two kinds. The first kind were those composite scores obtained by conflation from the observation records and described by their central tendencies in the tables in the section of this paper which reviews the classroom observations. Variables found insignificant at this first stage of search included most notably the domain of concern (Tables 11 and 22) and the simplicity-elaboration of the teachers' topic-relevant ratings (Table 15). The various groupings of affective solicitation (Tables 6 and 7) were also found not to be significant. The other sets of conflations each yielded one or more variables found to be significant at this stage.

The second kind of teacher-behaviour variables were derived variables, i.e. scores obtained not by conflation but by using the observation records in other ways. These derived scores are described in Table 26.

[1]While process-product studies 'have produced some of the best variables on the relationship between teacher behaviour and student achievement' (Rosenshine and Furst, 1971), they demand a pupil outcome measure. Siegel and Siegel (1967) have commented on the criterion inadequacies of instructional research, and the literature is by no means univocal on the value, definition and expression of criterion measures (Cronbach and Furby, 1970; O'Connor, 1972; Sjogren, 1970; Wittrock and Wiley, 1970).

Table 26: *Derived teacher-behaviour variables (observational data)*

(i) Regulative behaviour per hour. (Regulative reactions plus management solicitations.)

(ii) Regulative behaviour expressed as a percentage of all observed solicitations and reactions.

(iii) Reaction-variability. (Number of reaction categories employed.)

(iv) Instructional solicitations (S5 to 31) per hour.

(v) Proportion of vicariously-taught pupils. (Proportion of pupils present who were not the individual targets of any solicitation or reaction. Target-records used for this.)

In Table 26 the insignificance of solicitation-variability may be seen by its exclusion. The other derived teacher-behaviour variables which were not significant were (i) reactions per hour, (ii) instructional reactions per hour, and (iii) the ratio of instructional solicitation to instructional reaction.

Assessment-accuracy. Significant assessment-accuracy variables are shown in Table 27.

Table 27: *Measures of teachers' assessment-accuracy (paper-and-pencil tasks)*

---

1. *Teachers' Cognitive Assessments*
    (i) Accuracy coefficient. Autumn Ranking Task.
    (ii) Error. Autumn Ranking Task.
    (iii) Improvement in Accuracy coefficient. Ranking Task.
    (iv) Reduction in error. Ranking Task.
    (v) Error. Autumn Difficulty-index Task.
    (vi) Error. Autumn Norm-related comparisons.

2. *Teachers' Affective Assessments*
    (i) Error. High-ranked pupils' Attitudes to School. Autumn.
    (ii) Error. High-ranked pupils' Attitudes to English Lessons. Autumn.
    (iii) Error. High-ranked pupils' Attitudes to School. Summer.
    (iv) Error. High-ranked pupils' Attitudes to English. Summer.
    (v) Error. High-ranked pupils' Attitudes to English Lessons. Summer.

3. Scores on Test of Interpersonal Knowledge.

In Table 27, the loss to the final analysis of the teachers' summer scores on cognitive assessment tasks, and of the teachers' attitudinal assessments of their low-ranked pupils will be seen by their exclusion.

Inspection of those variables which were admitted to the final search suggested the existence of two major orthogonal factors, an attitude and an achievement factor. But no hypotheses were formally set up and the chosen array of variables was submitted to the second search (by principal components), the first four factors to be extracted and rotated to a terminal solution.

(c) Findings from the second stage of search

Ten factors accounted for all the variance, and the first four (accounting for 58·97 per cent of the variance) were subjected, as planned, to Varimax rotation. Variables which loaded at ·4 or above on the rotated factors appear in Tables 28 to 31. Only Factor Two (Table 29) may be labelled general-attitudinal, all the attitude measures loading highly on it. The three other factors have to do with the various measures of achievement.

Table 28: *Variables loading on rotated factor one (19·62% variance)*

	Loading	Pupil Variable
I	·40	Median shift in standardized achievement score.
		Teacher Variables
2	−·46	Error in summer predictions of high-ranked pupils' attitudes to School.
*3	·70	Number of instructional solicitations (S5 to 31) per hour.
*4	−·91	Management solicitations (S1) expressed as a percentage of all solicitations.
*5	·66	Probing questions (S20 to 25) expressed as a percentage of Instructional-interactional solicitations. (As in Table 8.)
*6	·44	Responding (R8) expressed as a percentage of affective modifiers (R7 to 12).
*7	·86	Positive ratings expressed as a percentage of all ratings (R15 to 34).
*8	−·86	Negative ratings expressed as a percentage of all ratings (R15 to 34).
*9	−·81	Historical achievement ratings (R31 and 32) expressed as a percentage of all reactions.
*10	−·94	Regulative ratings (R27 to 30, plus R33 and 34) expressed as a percentage of all reactions.
*11	−·75	Role ratings (R33 and 34) expressed as a percentage of all reactions.
*12	·90	Topic-relevant reactions (R1 to 26) expressed as a percentage of all reactions.
*13	−·90	Topic-irrelevant reactions (R27 to 35) expressed as a percentage of all reactions.
*14	−·86	Regulative behaviour (regulative reactions plus management solicitations) per hour.
*15	−·97	Regulative behaviour expressed as a percentage of all solicitations and reactions.

*These variables were obtained from the classroom observation data.

Table 29: *Variables loading on rotated factor two (13·99% variance)*

	Loading	Pupil Variables	
I	·80	Attitudes to School	
2	·90	Attitudes to English	*Mean shift*
3	·82	Attitudes to English Lessons	
4	·72	Attitudes to School	
5	·87	Attitudes to English	*Median shift*
6	·76	Attitudes to English Lessons	
		Teacher Variables	
*7	·45	'Synthesis' (S12) expressed as a percentage of cognitive taxonomized solicitations (S8 to 13).	
*8	·66	Complex cognitive solicitations (S12 and 13) expressed as a percentage of S8 to 13.	
*9	·48	Solicitations with clues (S1 to 28) expressed as a percentage of all solicitations.	
*10	−·48	Solicitations without clues (S29 to 31) expressed as a percentage of all solicitations.	
*11	·75	'Synthesis' (R5) expressed as a percentage of cognitive modifiers (R1 to 6).	
*12	·45	'Evaluation' (R6) expressed as a percentage of cognitive modifiers (R1 to 6).	
*13	·55	Reaction-variability.	

*These variables were obtained from the classroom observation data.

Table 30: *Variables loading on rotated factor three (13·89% variance)*

	Loading	Pupil Variables
I	·61	Mean shift in standardized achievement score.
2	·55	Median shift in standardized achievement score.
		Teacher Variables
3	·56	Error score on autumn Norm-Related Comparisons.
4	−·76	Accuracy coefficient. Autumn Ranking Task.
5	·83	Error score. Autumn Ranking Task.
6	·81	Improvement in accuracy coefficient over the year.
7	·79	Reduction in error score over the year.
*8	·83	'Knowledge' (S8) expressed as a percentage of cognitive taxonomized solicitations (S8 to 13).
*9	−·74	'Comprehension' (S9) expressed as a percentage of cognitive taxonomized solicitations (S8 to 13).
*10	·43	'Evaluation' (R6) expressed as a percentage of cognitive modifiers (R1 to 6).
*11	−·45	Evaluative ratings (R15 to 18) expressed as a percentage of all reactions.
*12	·82	Social responding (R35) expressed as a percentage of all reactions.
*13	−·40	Reaction-variability.

*These variables were obtained from the classroom observation data.

Table 31: *Variables loading on rotated factor four (11·48% variance)*

	Loading	Pupil Variable
I	−·54	Mean shift in standardized achievement score.
		Teacher Variables
2	−·40	Error score on the autumn Difficulty-Index Task.
*3	·45	'Synthesis' (S12) expressed as a percentage of cognitive taxonomized solicitations (S8 to 13).
*4	−·82	Positive regulative reactions expressed as a percentage of all regulative reactions (R27 to 30, plus R33 and 34).
*5	·82	Negative regulative reactions expressed as a percentage of all regulative reactions (R27 to 30, plus R33 and 34).
*6	−·83	Positive topic-irrelevant ratings expressed as a percentage of all topic-irrelevant ratings (R27 to 34).
*7	·83	Negative topic-irrelevant ratings expressed as a percentage of all topic-irrelevant ratings (R27 to 34).
*8	·40	Evaluative ratings (R15 to 18) expressed as a percentage of all reactions.
*9	·42	Reaction-variability.
*10	−·87	Proportion of vicariously-taught pupils.

*These variables were obtained from the classroom observation data.

(d) **Discussion**

(i) *Assessment-accuracy. Paper-and-pencil tasks*

Following TOTE, accurate testing precedes appropriate operation, and one would assume constant positive relationships between assessment-accuracy (measured in this study by the teachers' scores on the various paper-and-pencil assessment tasks) and the attainment of diverse teaching goals. However, this kind of measure was associated only with achievement. Further, loadings by these scores (variable 2 on Factor 1, variables 3 to 7 on Factor 3, and variable 2 on Factor 4) seem to suggest the importance of taking such accuracy measures over an extended period of time, since it was teachers' initial errors (i.e. inaccuracies), but subsequent reductions in error, which were positively associated with achievement.

From these loadings it seems to be the case that assessments which at the start of the academic year are chaotic and awry, but improve in accuracy over time, may be felicitous so far as certain achievement-outcomes are concerned. Such an interpretation of the findings would accord with the notions underlying expectancy research, since it suggests the utility of a teacher's inability (or reluctance) accurately to 'nail down' her pupils' statuses very early in the year.

The loadings also suggest the necessity for a phase-specific TOTE model in research which employs assessment-accuracy measures of this kind. His lack of phase-specific data, and his use of pupils' descriptions of their teachers as the pupil-variables, may explain the fruitlessness of Gage's (1955) search which reports that 'most of the correlations are essentially zero' and 'intercorrelations. . .revealed only one significant correlation. This was an r of ·28 between a teacher's accuracy in predicting inter-pupil preferences and her pupils' judgment that their teacher 'knows which pupil you like best in this class.' Gage's findings were from a 103-classroom study.

(ii) *Assessment-process. The classroom observations*

Comparisons between these data and those of other researchers are to be made with hesitation because no previous research has been similarly concerned with the study of on-going classroom testing acts. Also, where test acts have been included in observation-schedules, there are many definitional, coding-system and other discrepancies. However, certain comparisons do suggest themselves. Rosenshine (1971) has recently attempted to classify observation-studies into comparable-variable groupings. His review will be referred to and his caveat repeated: 'the reader should be aware that the definitions the investigators gave may not be comparable, and these definitions may not be identical to the operational definitions which the observers developed in the course of coding' (p.59).

(iii) *The obtained factors*

1. Factor one

Factor One (Table 28), containing median pupil-achievement shift, may be labelled an achievement-oriented or business-like factor. Here topic-relevant feedback (variable 12) loads positively. Conversely, feedback unrelated to the manifest topic of the lesson (variable 13) loads negatively. Other variables partially derived from (variables 14, 15) or subsumed by (variables 10, 11) this work-irrelevant composite, also load negatively, as does the work-irrelevant solicitation variable (variable 4) which appears.

Reviewing studies of this kind of business-like behaviour in teachers, Rosenshine (ibid, p.96) detects a 'consistent positive trend in favour' of it, and Kounin's work (1970), by defining classroom-management skill in terms of the absence of teachers' regulative work-irrelevant acts, also brings this kind of task-oriented proclivity to one's attention.

Probing-questioning (variable 5), another topic-centred composite, loads positively with achievement here as it has done in previous researches (Rosenshine, 1971). Also, that positive rather than negative general feedback (variables 7 and 8) loads positively here, finds support in the literature (ibid, p.59).

In sum, this factor reflects a generally positive but task-centred teacher, able to focus her solicitation and to give her feedback upon the topic here-and-now, to probe her pupils' responses to the topic, ignoring matters of achievement-history, avoiding work-irrelevancy and deviance, and, when offering modifying affective feedback, emitting this at a rather simple level.

2. Factor two

Few studies have used multiple-classification of questions, but those few report an association between high-level questioning and various measures of achievement. Rosenshine commends multiple-classification systems 'in which each type is first studied individually before the types are combined into ratios or composites' (ibid. p.131).

Multiple-classification was, of course, employed in the present study and it is high-level cognitive questioning (variables 7 and 8, Table 29) and high-level cognitive modifying feedback (variables 11 and 12) which appear in the general attitudinal factor. General variation in teacher-behaviour has not been a consistently promising variable in instructional research hitherto, but in this study reaction-variability associates positively with pupil-attitude. Clarity of solicitation (variables 10 and 11) also loads positively here. This is a different composite from the various topic-centred composites which loaded on the first (achievement) factor, since it subsumes some work-irrelevant solicitation (e.g. managerial and social), and measures classroom demands which though they may vary widely in their concerns, are expressed with clarity.

This factor suggests that pupils express generally positive feelings in classrooms in which the teacher is cognitively challenging and exciting (variables 7, 8, 11, 12) but not confusing or perplexing (variable 10), in which there may be some variety in the teacher's clearly stated demands (variable 9) and in which the teacher employs a variety of feedback modes.

3. Factors three and four

The composition of these achievement factors underlines the criterion difficulties in instructional research. Since it was the first achievement factor (Table 28) which contained median pupil-achievement shift, and accounted for the largest amount of variance, it is probably the one which is of greatest interest in a study of the Comprehensive School Common Course class. The two lesser achievement factors contain mean pupil achievement shift, a variable more likely to be affected by the extreme scores of a few pupils in the class. That teacher-behaviour may affect different sub-groups of learners differently has been discussed by Messick (in Wittrock and Wiley, 1970) and by Rosenshine (1971, p.126), the former asking: 'But suppose treatment A is better for certain kinds of students and treatment B better for other kinds of students?' and the latter suggesting: 'It is possible that better results could be obtained if investigators included means of sub-groups in their analyses'.

A similar difficulty is raised in medical education. Langsley and Aycrigg (1970) have doubted the propriety of accepting one model physician, one criterion of appropriate performance, in varied patient consultations, and observational study of doctors (Morrison and Cameron-Jones, 1972) suggests that different patterns of behaviour may be displayed towards different kinds of patients by doctors who are clinically effective.

For both Factors Three and Four reaction-variability loads negatively, as do evaluative ratings. Factor Three (Table 30), containing mean and median achievement-shift, reflects teachers' improvements in assessment-accuracy during the academic year (variables 6 and 7) from a baseline of inaccuracy (variables 3, 4, 5), and proportions of social-responding and high-level modifying cognitive feedback, but simplicity of cognitive solicitation (variables 8 and 9).

Similarly in Factor Four (Table 31), high-level cognitive solicitation (variable 3) is negatively associated with achievement. Since achievement-shift is here the mean, and likely to be affected by a few extreme scores, it is scarcely surprising, perhaps, to find it in positive association with a high proportion of vicariously-taught pupils (variable 10), with positive regulative behaviour (examples include 'The only ones who are sitting up nicely'), and with positive feedback in areas outside the here-and-now topic of the lesson (examples include 'You've always been quick with dictionaries').

(e) **Summary**

Process-product analyses have commonly used the class as the statistical unit. When the criterion pupil scores for this study were achievement means, more likely than the median to be affected by the extreme scores of a sub-group in the class, then the teacher's tendency verbally to ignore a large proportion of individual pupils in the class loaded the most highly.

Median achievement, a measure less likely to be affected by a few extreme scores, appears in the first and largest factor. This factor reflects the generally positive but topic-centred, business-like, cluster of teacher-behaviours consistently supported in the literature. This factor also contains probing-questioning, another variable well supported by previous research.

This topic-centred, orderly, achievement-oriented factor stands in marked contrast to the clear factor of general pupil-attitude. Here, the whole suggests a teacher who, though she makes her demands with clarity, may press for pupil-responses in widely ranging areas, seems cognitively intriguing, complex and arousing in solicitation and reaction, and displays a widely-ranging repertoire of feedback.

IV   CONCLUSIONS

This paper has reported various ways of investigating teachers' assessments of their pupils. Of course, test action is only one of many matters which are relevant to teaching. Teachers' operations (such as summarizing, exemplifying) and pupils' characteristics may well seem to have a greater claim as potent classroom factors to research. But the interest of this paper is assessment and how for teachers and for teacher-trainers it may usefully be studied. When, in this research, testing is defined in process-terms for observational purposes, the data seem at least as promising as those derived from the paper-and-pencil measures of testing-accuracy more usually employed by researchers. In giving plain descriptive maps

(Section I) or acting as contributory data (Section II) the observational findings are of interest in themselves. And in process-product searches (Section III) they yield patterns of hypotheses.

While no previous investigation has specifically set out to abstract, for detailed study, test acts in teacher-talk in classrooms, observational data on some facets of classroom testing have accumulated in the literature (Rosenshine, 1971) though they have been largely unconsidered in teachers' college courses on assessment. It is much more usual in such courses to teach trainees about formal assessment matters such as examining and grading.

And in assessment, as in psychology and other college courses which are assumed to be relevant to the classroom, the trainee gives, as evidence of skill, an end-of-course examination paper. But classroom studies suggest that teacher-trainers might also use observational viewpoints in assessment and in some other college courses (Aspy, 1972; Martin, 1972). Assessment skill may lie as much in what teachers say in classrooms as in their written assessments of their pupils.

This work was financed by a research grant
from the Scottish Education Department.

APPENDIX

The pupil measures
1. *The measurement of pupils' attitudes*

Pupils' attitudes to school, to English, and to their English Lessons were measured by three Likert-type scales assembled at first by the processes of adaptive plagiarism (Husén, 1967; Miller, 1961) and invention. First versions of the scales were piloted on 100 first-year pupils in a comprehensive school and from this study the discriminating items, supplemented by items contributed by the pupils, were presented to the pilot sample proper, of 200 Comprehensive pupils in another county. The final versions of the scales consisted of those items which had a reliability of ·85 or above, and which discriminated at least at the ·01 level. Each scale contains positive and negative items, randomly presented and scored from one to seven, the response categories ranging from Very Strongly Agree to Very Strongly Disagree. The strongest positive response on an item received a score of seven.

On each occasion the scales were completed by pupils after graphic and verbal instructions had been given by the researcher for two items not included in any of the scales.

The ATTITUDES TO SCHOOL scale consists of 17 items (e.g. 'School is rather boring most of the time'; 'I feel very happy when I am at school').

The ATTITUDES TO ENGLISH scale consist of 15 items (e.g. 'It is worth it to work very hard at English'; 'People who go in for English are less intelligent than scientists').

The ATTITUDES TO ENGLISH LESSONS scale consists of 17 items (e.g. 'I like talking to my teacher in English lessons'; 'I often feel confused during English').

The same scales were used throughout the studies. There were no titles on any of the scales.

2. *The measurement of pupils' achievement*

Bristol Achievement English Language Tests (Brimer, 1969) were used, level five being the appropriate test for Scottish schildren, who enter secondary school at the age of 12. Form A was used for the autumn test and Form B for the summer test.

3. *Obtaining the pupils' biographical data*

Biographical information about pupils was the criterion of accuracy on one of their teachers' assessment-tasks, i.e. the Interpersonal Knowledge Schedules. This information was obtained from the school records and by asking all the pupils to complete a simple biographical record (i.e. I have———sisters) which had been piloted earlier on 80 pupils in another county.

The teacher measures

The teachers were given blank copies of, and full information about, the measures used with their pupils, but were not at any stage given information about any pupil's score. First in the autumn term (after having taught their classes for approximately five weeks) and again at the end of the school year, the teachers performed various cognitive and affective assessment tasks. For each task there were full instructions, the task-sheets being assembled in booklet form with an introduction stressing that the teacher 'simply working in the light of your present knowledge of the children' should not consult the pupils or their records but should give personal impressions. The tasks were not timed, and took the following forms.

Cognitive assessments

1. Ranking Task. The task set was that of predicting the pupils' raw-score ranks on the Bristol Test. ('You should place a figure 1 beside the name of the pupil you think has probably got the highest total score, a figure 2 beside the pupil who you think has probably got the next highest total score, and so on, until all the listed pupils are dealt with.') The accuracy of these estimates was measured by using the pupils' rank-ordered scores as the criterion, disarray being expressed by mean distance ('Error') and by Spearman's rho ('Accuracy coefficient').

2. Difficulty-index Task. The Bristol Test consists of five parts, each designed to measure a different aspect of language achievement. These five subtests were listed and the teachers asked to rank them in order of difficulty for the class. ('You should place a figure 1 beside the part of the test which the class AS A CLASS may have done *the best*, a figure 2 beside the part . . . and so on . . . .') The criterion of accuracy for these predictions was the class's obtained rank order on the subtests. Disarray ('Error') was expressed by the sum of the squared differences. Tasks rather similar to 1 and 2 were presented to his subjects by Gage (1955).

3. Norm-related Comparisons. This task was that of predicting the achievement of the class against the achievements of the other classes in the sample, the teachers being told that these comprised Comprehensive Common Course pupils. Seven statements were presented (ranging from 'The class have probably done the best of all the classes on this test' to 'The class have probably done the worst of all the classes on this test'), the teacher to tick the statement which best expressed his estimate. This task was thought to make operational a comment made by Bronfenbrenner (1958) who, discussing the distinction to be made between 'sensitivity to the generalized other' and 'sensitivity to individual differences', added that 'a teacher may be keenly aware of individual differences among her

pupils yet completely overestimate, say, what an average fourth-grader can do.' The accuracy criterion for this task was a seven-banded rank order of all the classes in the sample, disarray ('Error') being expressed by squared distances.

Affective assessments
4. Prediction of pupils' responses on attitude scales. The teachers were asked to choose four pupils (These were those chosen by the teacher as the two most able in English and the two least able.) and to complete each of the three attitude scales for each chosen pupil 'as you guess that he or she has completed it'. The criterion of accuracy was pupil-response on each item, disarray ('Error'), being expressed by the mean of the summed distances on each scale.

Test of biographical information
5. Interpersonal Knowledge Schedule. A test of interpersonal information, given to the teachers in the spring term. A 14-item schedule was devised, each item soliciting factual and verifiable information about a pupil. Examples of items are: Name of pupil's Primary School; Number of brothers; Out-of-school clubs or organizations the pupil belongs to; Occupation of the pupil's father. The teachers completed a schedule for four pupils chosen by the teacher as the two most and the two least able in English. The criterion of accuracy on each item was the pupil's own auto biographical report and his school records, the teacher's score being the number of correct items. This post-dictive task was suggested by the work of Showell (1960), who used a similar instrument in his study of military leadership.

The observation schedule
6. A previous paper (Cameron-Jones, 1972) has described the making of this event-sampling schedule, designed to yield scores which describe a teacher's classroom assessment acts, the scores being the product of post-session elemental analysis by the researcher. Categorizing proceeds according to the rules (of present tense, singular number and positive occurrence) explicated by Medley and Mitzel (1963).

The element was chosen as the unit of analysis because classroom assessment acts sometimes occur, as it were parenthetically, within larger analytic units such as the move (Bellack, *et al.*, 1966) or incident (Nuthall and Lawrence, 1965). The element was the unit used also by Zahorik (1968) who assigned a category number 'to each part of the remark that represented a different feedback-element'.

The schedule's categories fall into two classes, (called solicitations and reactions) which appear to correspond to the stages of the two-phase process involved in any testing (see the introduction to this paper). Thus, in Biddle's terms (1967) the schedule would be described as a two-faceted coding system ('varieties of apples form a facet, but varieties of apples, oranges and elephants do not').

Solicitation and Reaction are of course the labels used by Bellack (1966) to describe two kinds of classroom-language move, and these terms were employed, despite the differences between Bellack's schedule and the one reported here, because the labels seemed, as generalizable organizers, to be of some descriptive value. Because they are descriptively inclusive the terms allow one to side-step, for example, such problems as precisely how an imperative (Broadie, 1972) or a 'question' is to be defined (Cohen, 1929).

Classroom assessment-events are considerably wider in their concerns ('Is your cold better now?') and in their forms (they may be non-verbal) than formal assessments, such as examinations, are. But there are also features common to both, and those elements which correspond to the components classified, largely as aids to formal assessment, by the taxonomists (Bloom, 1965; Krathwohl *et al.*, 1969), are categorized according to their schemes, though with matters of public record (e.g. 'Who wrote that poem ?': 'Where did Richard Hannay go after that ?') located on the schedule in the cognitive domain. Following Sanders (1966) all taxonomized assessments are coded at their highest level.

Since the schedule was to be used by a single researcher, reliability studies were concerned with the measurement of observer fidelity. First-wave reliability studies were carried out concurrently with the development of the schedule, by the Pearson Product-Moment formula and by the formula employed by Meux and Smith (1964) and also by De Landsheere (1969). Final measures of fidelity were obtained after code-recode[1] exercises, (recording after an eight-week interval) on 320 minutes of recorded teachers'-discourse, and, when fidelity was calculated separately for each category, Pearson coefficients from ·90 to unity were obtained. Despite this level of fidelity, all the tape recordings made for the present study were coded-recoded and 32 cases (in, for the most part, R14 and R19) of missed coding were thereby located for insertion in the observation records.

The schedule identifies 31 elements of solicitation and 37 of reaction. In the event, the 37 categories of reaction were not exhaustive, since they failed to accommodate the civility-elements (e.g. 'I'm so sorry', 'I apologise') observed during the research. Waismann has discussed (1945) the essential incompleteness of any empirical description, and he prepares the observationist rather well for a schedule's insufficiencies.

'. . . But however far I go, I shall never reach a point where my description will be completed: logically speaking, it is always possible to extend the description by adding some detail or another. Every description stretches, as it were, into a horizon of open possibilities: how far I go, I shall always carry this horizon with me. Contrast this case with others in which completeness is attainable. If, in geometry, I describe a triangle, e.g. by giving its three sides, the description is *complete:* nothing can be added to it that is not included in, or at variance with, the data.'

Applying the schedule. The schedule may be used in many ways, for example as a way of coding the assessment elements in sound and video-tape-recorded teaching. In the present study, for which the observation visits were made in the spring term, it was used for post-session coding of sound-tape-recordings, in conjunction with concurrent coding. Klein (1971) reports a rather similar modus operandi: 'During each experiment the verbal behaviours of the teacher was recorded by a concealed tape-recorder, while non-verbal behaviour was recorded by observers.'

Concurrent coding for the present study was of the silent categories, and of the pupil-target of each assessment, an individual pupil being identified by his number on a class-room seating plan: other pupil descriptions were 'Group' and 'Whole class'. Post-session analysis categorized, from the tape-recordings, each assessment element, and attached it to its pupil-target. A target was the pupil, or pupils, apparently attended to, e.g.

Teacher   'When was this written ?' (Whole class target)
         'Joyce ?' (Joyce is the target)
Joyce   'About a hundred years ago'.
Teacher   'Yes'. (Still looking at the same target child.)

---

[1]In elemental analyses, each coding decision can follow many replays of the relevant section of the tape—an advantage of any kind of post-session analysis.

The second section of this paper suggests that whole-class target-records are worth the making, but reliability (in this study between ·95 and unity on category S4, for concurrent target-record sheets compared with naming events extracted from the sound-tapes) demands an observer sufficiently familiar with the class to make accurate identifications of the pupils during diverse and very rapid interactions. Also, the teacher's vocative eccentricities (e.g. calling a pupil by her elder sister's name) are to be previously discriminated. Such constraints place limitations on one's sample size.

7. Pupils' opportunity to learn criterion material. In the summer term the teachers rated their classes' opportunity to learn the criterion achievement material by rating the face validity of the Bristol Test. Ratings were made on a six-point scale (From 'This test might almost have been designed with my pupils in mind' to 'This test has almost nothing to commend it for use with my pupils'), the teacher ticking the statement which best expressed his estimate. This variable was not intended as an assessment test but was used in the first-stage of the Process-Product analysis, and was not significant.

BIBLIOGRAPHY

ALLPORT, G. W. (1958). *The Nature of Prejudice.* New York: Doubleday.

ASPY, D. N. (1972). 'An investigation into the relationship between teachers' factual knowledge of learning theory and their classroom performance', *J. Teacher Educ.*, **23**, 1, 21–4.

AUSTIN, J. L. (1962). *How To Do Things with Words*, URMSON, J. O. (Ed.). Oxford: Clarendon Press.

BELLACK, A. A. *et al.* (1966). *The Language of the Classroom.* New York: Teachers' College Press.

BIDDLE, B. J. (1967). 'Methods and concepts in classroom research', *Rev. Educ. Res.*, **37**, 3, 337–57.

BLOOM, B. S. (Ed.) (1965). *A Taxonomy of Educational Objectives. Handbook 1. The Cognitive Domain.* New York: Longmans.

BRIGGS, D. (1970). 'The influence of handwriting on assessment', *Educ. Res.*, **13**, 1, 50–5.

BRIMER, A. (1969). *Bristol Achievement Tests. Interpretive Manual.* London: Nelson.

BROADIE, A. (1972). 'Imperatives', *Mind*, **81**, 322, 179–90.

BRONFENBRENNER, U. *et al.* (1958). 'The Measurement of Skill in Social Perception'. In McCLELLAND, D. C., *Talent and Society.* London: Van Nostrand.

BROPHY, J. E. and GOOD, T. L. (1970). 'Teacher's communication of differential expectations for children's classroom performance: some behavioural data', *J. Educ. Psychol.*, **61**, 5, 365–74.

CAMERON-JONES, M. (1972). In CHANAN, G. (Ed.) *Research Forum on Teacher Education.* Slough: NFER.

CAMPBELL, D. T. (1957). 'Factors relevant to the validity of experiments in social settings', *Psychol. Bull.*, **54**, 4, 297–312.

CARTER, R. S. (1952). 'How invalid are the marks assigned by teachers ?' *J. Educ. Psychol.*, **43**, 218–28.

COHEN, F. S. (1929). 'What is a question ?' *The Monist*, **39**, 350–64.

CORTIS, G. A. and DEAN, A. J. (1969). 'Teaching skills of probationary primary teachers', *Educ. Res.*, **12**, 3, 230–4.

CORTIS, G. A. and DEAN, A. J. (1972). 'Teaching skills of probationary primary teachers—a follow-up survey', *Educ. Res.*, **14**, 3, 200–3.

CRONBACH, LEE J. and FURBY, L. (1970). 'How should we measure 'change'—or should we ?' *Psychol. Bull.*, **74**, 68–80.

DAVIDSON, H. H. and LANG, G. (1960). 'Children's perceptions of their teachers' feelings toward them related to self-perception, school achievement and behaviour', *J. Exp. Educ.*, **29**, 2, 107–18.

DE LANDSHEERE, G. (1969). *Comment les Maitres Enseignent. Analyses des interactions verbales en classes.* Brussels: Ministère de l'education nationale, administration des Etudes.

DUTHIE, J. H. (1970). *Primary School Survey*. Edinburgh: HMSO.

EGGLESTON, J. F. and KELLY, P. J. (1969). 'The assessment of project work in A-level biology', *Educ. Res.*, **12**, 3, 225–9.

EGGLESTON, J. F. and KERR, J. F. (1969). *Studies in Assessment*. London: English Universities Press.

FESHBACH, N. D. (1969). 'Student teacher preferences for elementary pupils varying in personality characteristics', *J. Educ. Psychol.*, **60**, 2, 126–32.

FLANDERS, N. A. *et al.* (1968). 'Changes in pupil attitudes during the school year', *J. Educ. Psychol.*, **50**, 5, 334–8.

GAGE, N. L. *et al.* (1955). 'Teachers' understanding of their pupils and pupils' ratings of their teachers', *Psychol. Monogr.* 406, **69**, 21, 1–37.

GOSLIN, D. A. (1967). *Teachers and Testing*. New York: Russell-Sage.

HADLEY, S. T. (1954). 'A school mark—fact or fancy?' *Educational Administration and Supervision*, **40**, 305–12.

HALLWORTH, H. J. (1964). 'Personality ratings of adolescents: A study in a comprehensive school', *Brit. J. Educ. Psychol.*, **34**, 171–7.

HIRST, P. H. (1971). 'What is teaching?' *J. Curric. Studies*, **3**, 1, 5–18.

HUCK, S. and BOUNDS, W. (1972). 'Essay grades: an interaction between graders handwriting clarity and the neatness of examination papers', *Amer. Educ. Res. J.*, **9**, 2, 279–83.

HUGHES, M. (1965). In AMIDON, E. and SIMON, A. 'Teacher-pupil interaction', *Rev. Educ. Res.*, **35**, 2, 130–9.

HUSEN, T. (Ed.) (1967). *International Study of Achievement in Mathematics. Vol. 1.* London: Wiley.

KLEIN, S. S. (1971). 'Student influence on teacher-behaviour', *AERA Journal*, **8**, 3, 403–21.

KOUNIN, J. S. (1970). *Discipline and Group Management in Classrooms*. London: Holt, Rinehart and Winston.

KRATHWOHL, D. R. *et al.* (1969). *A Taxonomy of Educational Objectives. Handbook 2. The Affective Domain.* New York: David Mackay.

LANGSLEY, D. G. and AYCRIGG, J. B. (1970). 'Filmed interviews for testing clinical skills', *J. Med. Educ.*, **45**, 52–8.

McHENRY, R. (1971). 'New methods of assessing the accuracy of interpersonal perception', *J. Th. Soc. Behav.*, **1**, 2, 109–19.

MARTIN, F. (1972). 'The effects of a creative problem-solving workshop upon the cognitive operations of verbal classroom interaction in the primary school grades', *Psychology in the Schools*, **9**, 2, 126–30.

MEDLEY, D. M. and MITZEL, H. E. (1963). 'Measuring Classroom Behaviour by Systematic Observation'. In GAGE, N. L. (Ed.) *Handbook of Research on Teaching*. Chicago: Rand McNally.

MEICHENBAUM, D. H., BOWERS, K. S. and ROSS, R. R. (1969). 'A behavioural analysis of teacher expectancy effect', *J. Pers. Soc. Psychol.*, **13**, 4, 306–16.

MELTZER, S. (1971). 'Teacher bias in pupil evaluation: A critical analysis', *J. Teacher Educ.*, **22**, 1, 40–3.

MEUX, M. and SMITH, B. O. (1964). 'Logical Dimensions of Teaching Behaviour'. In BIDDLE, B. J. *et al.*, *Contemporary Research on Teacher Effectiveness*. New York: Holt, Rinehart and Winston.

MILLER, G. A. *et al.* (1960). *Plans and the Structure of Behaviour*. New York: Holt, Rinehart and Winston.

MILLER, T. W. G. (1961). *Values in the Comprehensive School*. Edinburgh: Oliver and Boyd.

MORRISON, A. *et al.* (1965). 'Teachers' personality ratings of pupils in Scottish primary schools', *Brit J. Educ. Psychol.*, **35**, 306–19.

MORRISON, A. and CAMERON-JONES, M. (1972). 'A procedure for training for general practice', *Brit. J. Med. Educ.*, **6**, 125–32.

NUTHALL, G. A. and LAWRENCE, P. J. (1965). *Thinking in the Classroom*. Wellington: New Zealand Council for Educational Research.

O'CONNOR, E. F. (1972). 'Extending classical test theory to the measurement of change', *Rev. Educ. Res.*, **42**, 1, 73–97.

OJEMANN, R. H. and WILKINSON, F. R. (1939). 'The effect on pupil growth of an increase in teachers' understanding of pupil behaviour', *J. Exper. Educ.*, **8**, 143–7.

PENFOLD, D. M. and MELDON, R. P. (1969). 'Social sensitivity in relation to teaching competence', *Educ. Res.*, **12**, 64–6.

ROMMETVEIT, R. (1960). *Selectivity, Intuition and Halo Effects in Social Perception*. Oslo: Oslo University Press.

ROSENSHINE, B. (1971). *Teaching Behaviours and Student Achievement*. Slough: NFER.

ROSENSHINE, B. and FURST, N. (1971). 'Research on Teacher Performance Criteria'. In SMITH, B. O. (Ed.) *Research on Teacher Education: A symposium*. New Jersey: Englewood Cliffs.

RUNKEL, P. J. (1964). In GAGE, N. L. (Ed.) *A Handbook of Research on Teaching*. Chicago: Rand-McNally (page 126).

SANDERS, N. M. (1966). *Classroom Questions: What Kinds?* New York: Harper and Row.

SARBIN, T. R., TAFT, R. and BAILEY, D. E. (1960). *Clinical Inference and Cognitive Theory*. New York: Holt, Rinehart and Winston.

SEARLE, J. R. (1969). *Speech Acts. An Essay in the Philosophy of Language*. London: Cambridge University Press.

SHOWELL, M. (1960). 'Interpersonal knowledge and rated leader potential', *J. Abnorm. Soc. Psychol.*, **61**, 1, 87–92.

SIEGEL, L. and SIEGEL, L. C. (1967). 'A multivariate paradigm for instructional research', *Psychol. Bull.*, **68**, 5, 306–26.

SIEGEL, S. (1956). *Nonparametric Statistics for the Behavioural Sciences*. Maidenhead:McGraw-Hill.

SILBERMAN, M. L. (1969). 'Behavioural expression of teachers' attitudes toward elementary school students', *J. Educ. Psychol.*, **60**, 5, 402–7.

SJOGREN, D. A. (1970). 'Measurement techniques in evaluation', *Rev. Educ. Res.*, **40**, 2, 301–20.

WAISMANN, F. (1945). 'Verifiability', *Proceedings of the Aristotelean Society*, Suppl. Vol. 19, 119–50.

WARR, P. B. and KNAPPER, C. (1968). *The Perception of People and Events*. London: Wiley.

WILLEMS, E. P. and RAISH, H. L. (Eds.). (1969). *Naturalistic Viewpoints in Psychological Research*. New York: Holt, Rinehart and Winston.

WITTROCK, M. C. and WILEY, D. E. (Eds.). (1970). *The Evaluation of Instruction. Issues and Problems*. London: Holt, Rinehart and Winston.

ZAHORIK, J. A. (1968). 'Classroom feedback behaviour of teachers', *J. Educ. Res.*, **62**, 4, 147–50.

Analysis of Verbal Interaction in the Classroom

Gilbert De Landsheere
Head of the Department of Educational Research,
University of Liège, Belgium[1]

In this paper,[2] the system of interaction analysis developed in the Department of Edutional Research of the University of Liège is presented. Then six research projects completed by the author or under his supervision are abstracted. He concludes with a brief description of the beginnings of a new method of researching the pre-school child.

I THE CATEGORY SYSTEM

Background of the system

The basic idea of the author's system comes from M. Hughes and associates (1959). At first, a straightforward French translation was tried, but it soon appeared that Hughes' categories were neither exhaustive nor mutually exclusive. After analysing several thousand pieces of teacher behaviour, a new system (described hereunder) was developed; each function is operationally defined.

Though the words used are in many cases similar, the difference from Hughes' system is considerable: four out of Hughes' seven categories have been thoroughly revised; one has been rejected; three have been added; M. Hughes *et al*. identify 28 specific functions; we have 40; 14 functions only are common to both systems.

Why a very analytical approach?

It seems that the high complexity of teacher-pupil interactions make a very analytical approach necessary, whatever the consequences may be in terms of coding load, length of observers' training and reliability.

The weakness of gross systems is illustrated by N. Flanders' well-known category three in his non-expanded system ('Accepts or uses ideas of student'), which in fact

[1]For further information about the projects mentioned in this paper, readers may write to Professor G. De Landsheere, Laboratoire de Pédagogie expérimentale, Université de Liège au Sart Tilman, par 4,000 Liege 1, Belgium.

[2]Part of this paper has been published in the *Classroom Interaction Newsletter* (1971). Philadelphia, Penn.: Research for Better Schools, Inc., whose permission to republish we gratefully acknowledge.

covers behaviour categories as divergent (in terms of the author's system) as: development, imposition and positive feedback and, within this last category, feedback stereotype, repeat, specific, other.

One of the main factors explaining the general failure of research trying to relate teacher behaviour to pupil achievement is the crudeness of the independent variables used.

Face validity of the categories

Since a clear and educationally significant relationship (that is, long-term relationship) has not yet been satisfactorily demonstrated and measured between teacher behaviour and pupil achievement, one has to rely mainly upon the face validity of a category system.

We suggest that it should be observed in the first place whether the teacher keeps the classroom situation under sufficient *control:* beyond a certain level, democracy becomes *laissez faire,* or even anarchy. In this case, efficient (individual or group) work is practically impossible.

Furthermore, attention should be focused on two behaviour categories corresponding to the two main features of democratic education: for one thing, initiating the pupil into the existing culture (values, knowledge, skills, way of life etc.), which implies *imposition,* and, another, giving him the opportunity to become an *independent* adult, which implies liberty, critical thinking and so forth.

Facilitating and *reinforcing* functions have also to be considered. All factors of reinforcement are not yet accurately identified, but we know enough to recognize the necessity of reinforcement of pupil behaviour by the teacher.

Outline of the De Landsheere system

I   *Controlling functions*

Within this category, all functions creating favourable conditions for teaching or ordered working are grouped. These functions do not bear on subject matter, on substantive meaning.

1. Regulates pupils' participation (open; closed; global; neutral; justified choice).
2. Controls movements in the classroom. (Indicates where to go; authorizes move; does the move himself.)
3. Controls implementation of work. (Indicates lay-out; sequences; neutral control of work progress.)
4. Judges in cases of altercations or conflicts of interest.

II   *Impositive functions*

This category concerns subject matter only. The teacher is the one who decides upon the choice of subject matter, problems to be solved, and even response content and form.

1. Imposes information (lectures, answers his own questions).
2. Imposes problems.
3. Imposes the problem-solving method.
4. Gives cues.
5. Imposes opinion or value judgment.
6. Imposes help.

III   *Content developing functions*

Basically the teacher responds to data placed in the situation by the pupils.

    1.   Stimulates. (Creates stimulating conditions: suggests three or more activity choices.)

    2.   Invites independent research.

    3.   Structures. (Clarifies pupils' spontaneous statements; invites to clarify, develop, generalize, summarize, etc.; suggests an experimental control; invites pupil to state opinion.)

    4.   Meets requests for help. (Solves problem himself; guides pupil's research; gives information wanted.)

IV   *Functions of personal responses*

    1.   Welcomes a spontaneous participation.

    2.   Invites pupil to tell or report about personal experiences out of school.

    3.   Clarifies personal problem.

    4.   Individualizes teaching.

V   *Functions of positive feedback to pupils*

These functions bear on subject matter only: the pupils are informed of the validity of their answers or problem-solving behaviour.

    1.   Approves—stereotype.

    2.   Approves by repeating pupil's answer.

    3.   Approves specifically.

    4.   Others.

VI   *Functions of negative feedback*

    1.   Disapproves—stereotype.

    2.   Disapproves by repeating pupil's answer ironically or in accusing tone.

    3.   Disapproves specifically.

    4.   Feedback delayed.

    5.   Others.

VII   *Functions of concretization*

Since the focus is on verbal interactions, it is not the use of teaching aids that is observed, but the related functions. Methodologically, this category is a weakness in the system for it is not mutually exclusive with 'imposition' and 'development'. A specific evaluation of the concrete approach at primary school level seemed important enough to justify a double coding.

    1.   Uses material (figural representation; symbolic representation; construction).

    2.   Invites pupil to use material.

    3.   Audio-visual aids (used by teacher; by pupil).

    4.   Writes on the blackboard.

VIII   *Functions of positive affectivity*

This is an evaluation of the pupils' behaviour independent of specific subject matter.

    1.   Praises, mentions as a good example for others.

    2.   Solicits.

   3. Encourages.
   4. Promises reward.
   5. Rewards.
   6. Shows sense of humour.
   7. Words of affection ('dear', 'honey', etc.).

IX *Functions of negative affectivity*

   1. Criticizes, accuses, uses sarcasm.
   2. Threatens.
   3. Admonishes.
   4. Reprimands.
   5. Punishes.
   6. Postpones (e.g. P: 'May I show you my drawing?', T: 'No, not now: later on.').
   7. Negative personal response.
   8. Is cynical.

II RESEARCH OF G. DE LANDSHEERE WITH ASSISTANCE OF E. BAYER (1969)

In this research, special effort was made to control as many factors as possible:

   1. Level: 50 first grade periods (i.e. first form of elementary school in Belgium: six-year-olds).
   2. Population:
(a) Balanced sample of schools located in the different socio-economic quarters of Liège City and suburbs.
(b) 25 teachers randomly chosen.
   3. Type of period observed: discussion on an activity theme. Each teacher was observed during two 30-minute periods. For the first period, the teacher was left entirely free; for the second period, all teachers agreed to organize interactions around the same theme: 'We play with a magnet';
   4. Time of observation: on a Thursday between 9.30 and 10 a.m.;
   5. Reliability of coding of tape-recorded lessons: lower limit tolerated ·85; mostly above ·90.

The results appear in Table 1.

Table 1: *Instances of categorized behaviours observed in the 50 periods*

	Control	Imposition	Development	Personal responses	Feedb. +	Feedb. −	Concretization	Affect. +	Affect. −
n	5,931	7,568	452	815	2,498	592	2,925	304	844
%	27·0	34·5	2·1	3·7	11·4	2·7	13·3	1·4	3·8

For the 50 lessons together, 21,929 instances of the various teaching behaviours were identified. A high correlation was observed between the 25 profiles of the imposed theme activities (Kendall $W = ·84$), between the 25 profiles of free themes activities ($W = ·84$) and between the 50 profiles together ($W = ·83$). (See Figure 1.)

Such a high correlation might be caused by a lack of sensitivity of the instrument. However, when we observed a teacher, in another city, who practiced the Freinet type of project method, substantial differences appeared (see Figure 2).

Other results

1.   Though the Belgian primary school curriculum has been considered as one of the most progressive in the world since 1936, one observes that classroom instruction is definitely teacher centred:

Controlling functions	27·0%
Impositive functions	34·5%
Concretization by teacher	9·6%
	71·1%

2.   Some subcategories provide striking information:

(a) Only in 225 cases out of 21,929 is the pupil invited to refer to his extra-school experience;

(b) Only 8·2 per cent of the positive feedback functions are specific; 27·7 per cent of the negative feedback functions are specific;

(c) No case of use of audio-visual techniques was observed;

(e) Only in seven cases was the teacher's display of a sense of humour observed.

(d) Only in 26 cases was a pupil concretely rewarded;

(f) Only four cases of punishment were observed;

(g) A five-minute random sample of each lesson would have been representative of the whole session. This observation is, however, qualified in another research.

III   G. DE LANDSHEERE. Contrasted analysis of a five-minute random sample from one of the 50 lessons mentioned above with the N. Flanders (non-expanded) and the De Landsheere system.

The five-minute sample contained exactly 103 functions.

		Flanders' categories		
TEACHER	Indirect Influence	3. Accepts or uses ideas of student	13%	
		4. Asks questions	30%	43%
	Direct Influence	5. Lecturing or rhetorical questions	2%	
		6. Directions	11%	20%
		7. Criticizing or justifying authority	7%	
PUPIL		8. Student Talk—response	17%	
		9. Student Talk—initiation	18%	

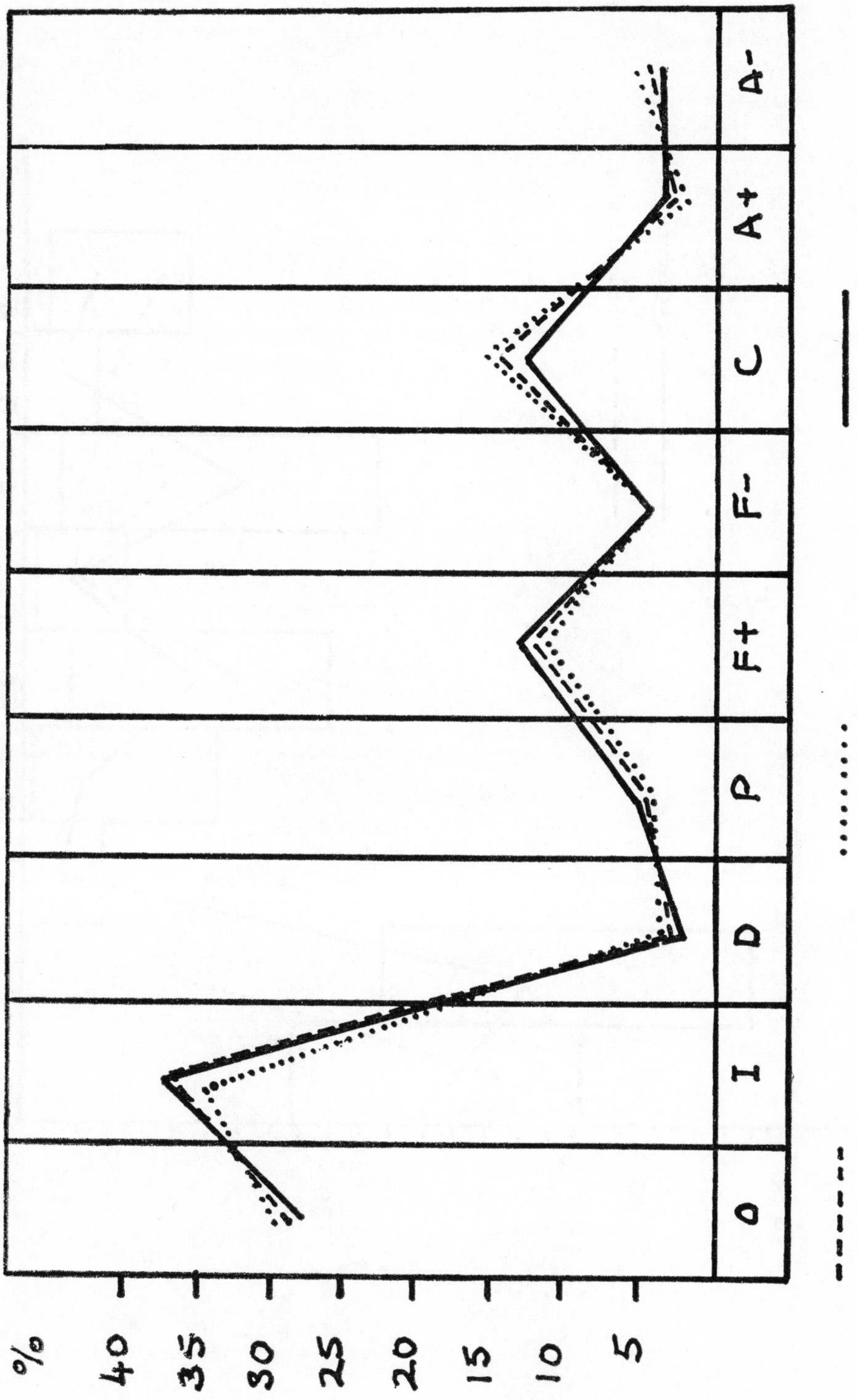

Figure 1 : *Profiles of 50 lessons, showing frequencies of the nine teaching categories*

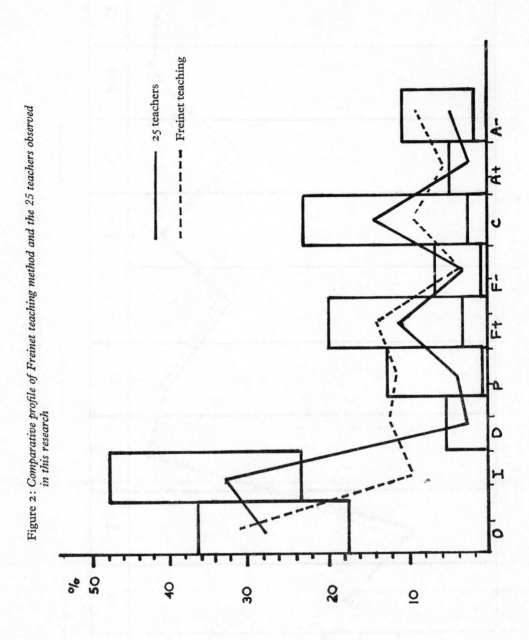

Figure 2: *Comparative profile of Freinet teaching method and the 25 teachers observed in this research*

The same sample coded according to the author's system led to the following results:

1. Control — 22%
2. Imposition — 27%
3. Development — —
4. Personal responses — 12%
5. Positive feedback — 15%
6. Negative feedback — 7%
7. Concretization — 7% (5% of which are teacher-initiated)
8. Positive affectivity — 5%
9. Negative affectivity — 5%

The analysis according to Flanders' matrix appears in Figure 3.

Figure 3: *Analysis of a five-minute random sample according to Flanders' matrix*[1]

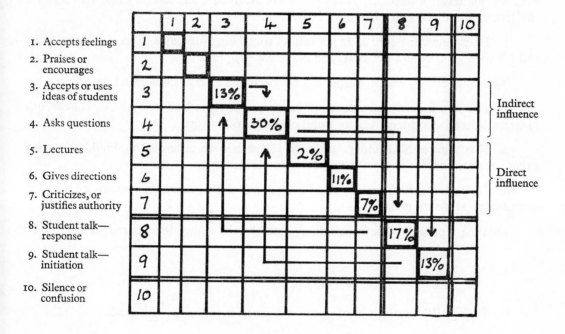

[1]See FLANDERS, N. E. (1966). *Interaction Analysis in the Classroom.* Ann Arbor: University of Michigan.

The explanation of the arrows is as follows: to code the series 10, 6, 10, 7, 5, 1, 4, 8, 4, 10, the numbers are tallied in the matrix, one pair at a time. The row is used for the first number, the column for the second number. The first pair is 10–6, so the tally is placed in the cell where row 10 joins column 6. The second pair 6–10; tally this in row 6, column 10. Each pair overlaps with the next. If one tallies without lifting the pencil, the main itineraries appear. These main routes are indicated by the arrows.

The following observations can be made:

1. While the Flanders system suggests that the sample analysed is pupil-centred ('Indirect influence', 43 per cent, plus 'Category nine', 18 per cent = 61 per cent pupil-centred), our system indicates a teacher-centred situation (Control, 20 per cent plus Imposition, 27 per cent plus five per cent of concretization = 54 per cent teacher-centred).

2. Flanders' category three corresponds at least to our categories III and V:

Flanders 13 per cent;
De Landsheere 15 per cent (but category III in this case = 0).

So, in the present sample, what Flanders calls 'Accepts or uses pupil's ideas' is exclusively 'positive feedback' in our system. A further analysis shows that all positive feedback functions belong to the sub-category 'feedback repeat': no one case of specific feedback exists in the sample. This is an example (though we cannot conclusively generalize from this one observation) of how misleading a rather gross analysis can be.

3. In this case, Flanders' category seven (seven per cent) corresponds exactly to what we call negative feedback (seven per cent). Normally, our category No. IX (negative affectivity) would also enter Flanders' No. seven.

4. To explain our figure of 22 per cent of controlling functions, it seems that we must add Flanders' No. six (11 per cent) and No. eight (17 per cent).

This comparison, which, purposely, has been made very simple, suggests:

1. That two widely used systems of interaction analysis lead to dissimilar conclusions in terms of 'teacher centred' versus 'pupil centred' instruction.

2. That some of N. Flanders' categories (especially three and four) should be refined to convey a clearer idea of what is happening in the classroom.

3. That after some revision, the Flanders and De Landsheere systems could most probably be made compatible.

Figure 4 represents a new matrix suggested by the author for this purpose.

IV   G. JACQUES, Analysis of 76 geography periods, in the seventh grade

Total of instances identified: 11,333.
Duration of total observation: 800 minutes.
Rate: ± 1 function/4″.

As shown on the following profiles (Figure 5), the overall results for geography are very similar to those obtained with the 25 first grade teachers studied earlier. The range of the geography teachers is much smaller in all categories.

In this case, and with the exception of the first 10 minutes, each 10-minute sub-sample has no lower correlation with the whole period than ·83.

Figure 4: *Suggested new matrix**

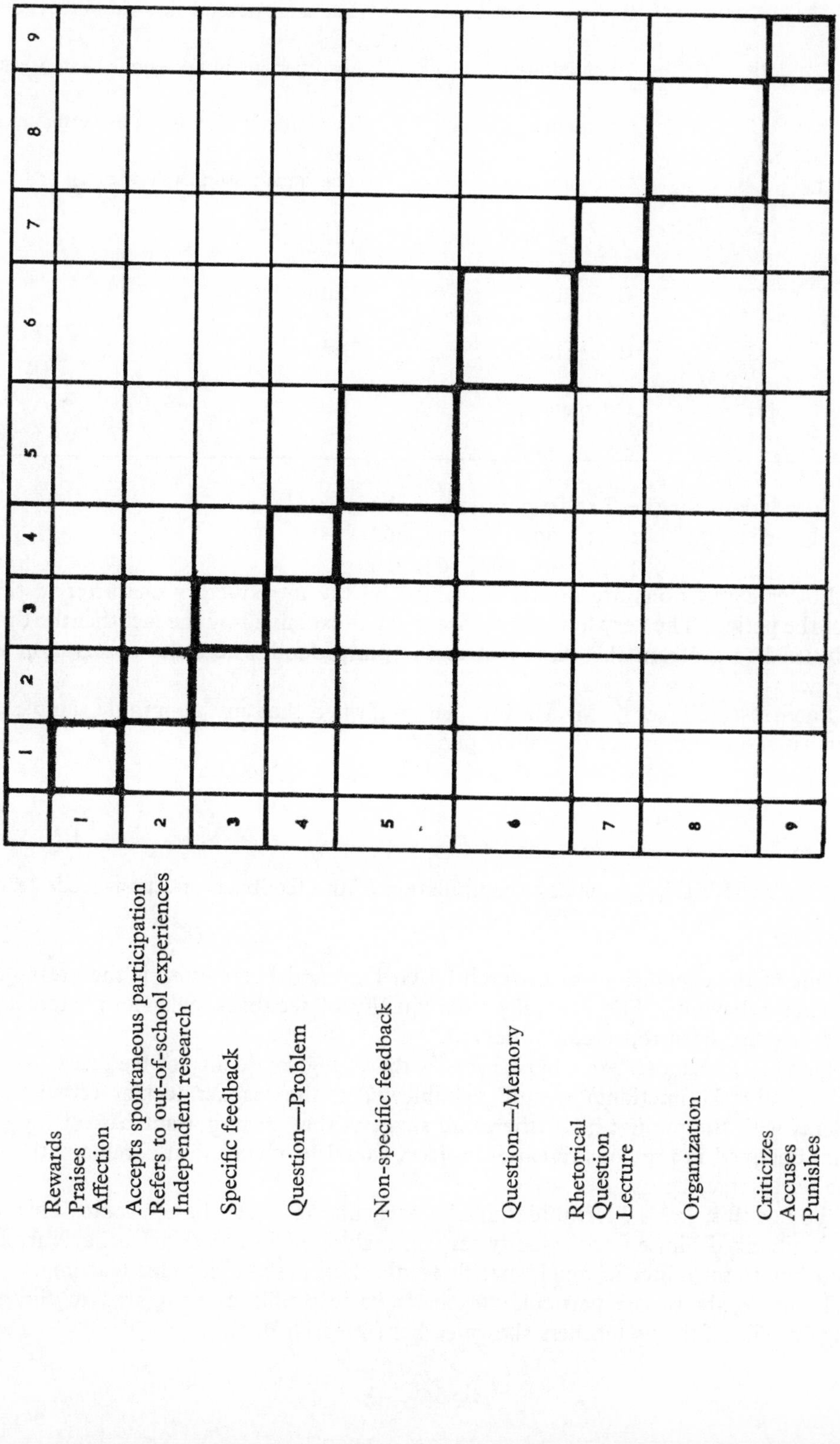

*The sizes of the cells are in proportion to the most commonly observed frequencies

No.	Teacher	Topic	Remark
1 2	A	Relief	The same lesson twice with different classes.
3 4	B	Orientation	Two periods in the same class a week apart
5 6	C	Orientation	Two different lessons in two different classes
7 8	D	Orientation	The same lesson twice with different classes
9 10	E	Types of farm buildings in Belgium	Ditto
11 12	F	Orientation	Ditto
13 14	G	Orientation	Ditto
15 16	H	Orientation	Ditto

Correlations for the first 10-minute samples are:
·62; ·82; ·93; ·83; ·99; ·97; ·75; ·62;
·98; ·42; ·97; ·70; ·95; ·90; ·65; ·19.

Lower correlations are mostly explained by the introductory character of the first part of the period. The very low correlation of ·19 is explained by the fact that the time was mostly used to go from the classroom to the playground where the observation was to take place.

Later research (see J. M. Martin), has confirmed that any 10-minute sample except the first is representative of the whole period.

V   J. M. MARTIN, Systematic manipulation of the feedback of a first-grade teacher

One of the conclusions of research by G. De Landsheere *et al.* is the great stability of teacher behaviour. The generally poor quality of feedback behaviour (stereotype or repeat) has also been repeatedly observed.

One of De Landsheere's hypotheses is that a higher quality of feedback (that is, of specific feedback functions) is only possible when the teacher tackles rather complex problems with the pupils; he furthermore suggests that an important part of the general profiles obtained in previous research projects would be changed in parallel with changes in the feedback category.

To test this, J. M. Martin identified a particular teacher's basic profile. This teacher then familiarized himself with our system of analysis of instructional behaviour, and we invited him to introduce as much specific feedback as possible into his teaching.

Figure 6 shows the particular teacher's basic profile as compared to the general average profile of the 25 teachers shown earlier (research B, above).

Figure 5: *Profiles for 76 geography periods—averages and ranges*

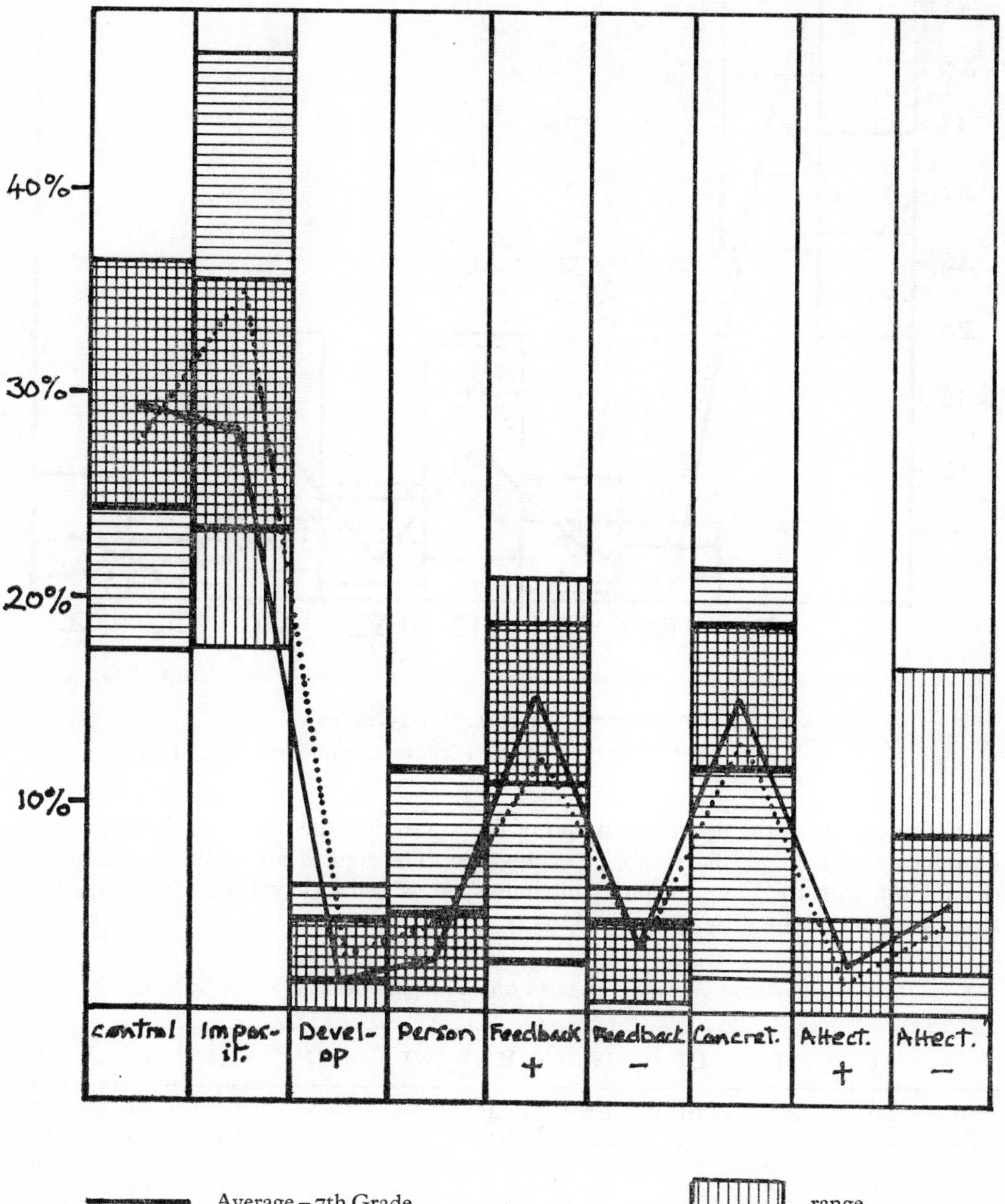

Average – 7th Grade
Average – 1st Grade

range

range

Control

Figure 6: *Profile of individual teacher compared with 25 teachers*

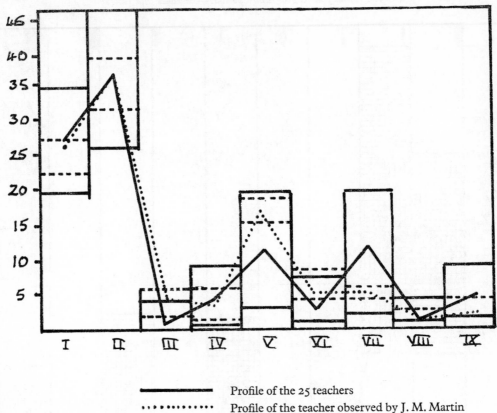

```
              Profile of the 25 teachers
  • • • • • • • • •   Profile of the teacher observed by J. M. Martin
```

Table 2 shows the new distribution of functions after the teacher had been asked to introduce as much specific feedback as possible. The figures are given for six periods (B1 to B6), with the nine categories distinguished as usual. It will be remembered that feedback is represented by category V.

Table 2: *Distribution of teacher functions with maximized feedback (in percentages)*

	I	II	III	IV	V	VI	VII	VIII	IX	N
B1	24·1	31·7	7·1	4·7	19·2	4·6	3·6	3·5	1·6	548
B2	25	31·5	5·9	4·2	18·4	4·4	5·2	2·9	2·5	613
B3	30·2	31·9	7·8	1·7	19	3·5	3·5	1·7	0·9	116
B4	23·5	33·6	4·2	8·4	20·2	3·4	3·4	1·7	1·7	119
B5	25·5	40	3	4·9	16·4	2·4	4·9	1·8	1·2	165
B6	28·2	34·8	5·3	4·4	18·7	2·6	3	1·3	1·5	529

Table 3 shows the distribution of feedback functions in six periods (A1 to A6) *before* the experiment; and Table 4 shows the comparable functions in the six observed periods after the teachers had been asked to intensify the feedback.

Table 3: *Feedback before the experiment (in percentages)*

	Stereotype	Repeat	Specific	Other	N
A1	14·7	78·9	1·8	4·6	109
A2	13·6	77·3	—	9·1	22
A3	2·8	86·1	2·8	8·3	36
A4	7·1	89·3	—	3·6	28
A5	17·1	77·1	1·4	4·3	70
A6	9·3	86·7	—	4	75

Table 4: *Feedback in the experimental periods*

	Stereotype	Repeat	Specific	Other	N
B1	10·5	66·7	20	2·8	105
B2	6·2	68·1	21·2	4·5	113
B3	18·2	59·1	18·2	4·5	22
B4	8·3	70·8	20·8	—	24
B5	22·2	70·4	7·4	—	27
B6	13·1	72·7	11·1	3·1	99

J. M. Martin's experience leads to the following observations:

1. The total number of feedback functions did not vary significantly.

2. The teacher was able to increase significantly his number of specific feedback functions; the feedback-repeat functions decreased approximately in the same proportion.

3. However, two qualifications must be made:

(a) The increase of specific feedback functions mainly took place in the first 20 minutes of the period.
Hypothesis one: Complex problems calling for specific feedback appear when the fundamental features of the lesson are introduced; the second part of the period is mainly focused on applications and drill, less favourable to high level feedback.
Hypothesis two: Once he gets a bit tired, the teacher comes back to former routine.

(b) After a few experimental periods, it was observed that the number of specific feedback functions decreased; the trend was to come back to the pre-experimental situation.
Hypothesis one: Habits are strong and a sort of long educational therapy might be needed to change a teacher's behaviour.
Hypothesis two: The way we obtained more specific feedback was superficial. Feedback behaviour cannot be isolated from the whole pattern of instruction. This whole pattern must be changed (for instance, from teacher-centred to pupil-centred instruction) if we want a lasting and functional modification of the feedback behaviour.

4. A definite relation has been shown with specific feedback: imposition (negative); development (positive).

5. Specific feedback generally follows interactions, including an analysis of the situation.

6. This, of course, is an exploratory research. Its results cannot be generalized. The only purpose is to show that the basic hypotheses are worth further endeavour.

VI   A. M. NINANE, Analysis of teaching sessions on arithmetical problems, with the B. Bloom *et al.* taxonomy of educational objectives, cognitive domain—sixth grade

Though no evaluative judgement had been made with the De Landsheere system, it seemed that the profile generally obtained was a symptom of rather poor teaching. To test this hypothesis, a type of activity which seemed favourable for higher mental processes was selected: arithmetical problems.

Number of sixth grade teachers observed: nine.

Duration of observation: 432 minutes.

Number of functions identified: 1,272.

Table 5: *Analysis of nine teachers' behaviour according to Bloom's taxonomy*

Teacher No.	Taxonomy level*					
	I	II	III	IV	V	VI
1	33	35	8	3	6	12
2	34	30	10	7	3	17
3	42	31	15	–	1	11
4	44	37	15	–	–	4
5	38	35	25	–	–	2
6	55	23	19	–	–	4
7	37	48	13	–	–	3
8	40	38	17	1	–	4
9	65	16	13	–	–	9

*I = Knowledge   IV = Analysis
II = Comprehension   V = Synthesis
III = Application   VI = Evaluation

Average

I	II	III	IV	V	VI
43%	33%	15%	1%	1%	7%

Conclusions

For all teachers observed, the two lower levels of the taxonomy play the main role (average: 76 per cent).

For seven teachers out of nine, practically no analysis or synthesis eliciting functions are observed.

The general hypothesis of low quality teaching is confirmed.

VII E. BAYER, *Multidimensional Analysis of Verbal Communication in the Classroom*, Univ. of Liège. Unpublished doctoral dissertation, 1972.

A look at this last decade's research in the field of classroom interaction analysis reveals a definite progress but also a strong limitation in the many systems experimented. This limitation is mainly due to the fact that, owing to their own field of interest or to their idiosyncrasies, most authors have chosen to study one single dimension of the teaching process.

This process is complicated enough to justify such a partial approach. However, the time has come for the development of more comprehensive systems or, at least, for multidimensional studies of the same educational reality.

E. Bayer's approach belongs to this new trend. He has developed a set of systems where the influence of three main orientations is distinctly felt: G. De Landsheere's system of *Classroom Interaction Analysis*, A. Bellack's system for the study of *Language in the Classroom*, and B. Bloom's *Taxonomy of Educational Objectives, Cognitive Domain*.

Bellack's categories are used without much change to analyse the basic functions of communication.

Bloom's taxonomy is simplified along the lines of Aschner and Gallagher, and the categories[1] are used to identify the cognitive level of the information taught and of the activities generated in the classroom.

De Landsheere's categories, in some cases modified, are resorted to with a view to the characterizing of crucial aspects of instruction: organization and control of school life, transmission or discovery of knowledge and attitudes, and psychological climate of teacher-pupil interaction.

The *sentence* was chosen as basic unit for the analysis of verbal behaviour. Among other things, it seemed that the number of sentences used in relation to a specific topic could be considered an index of the importance of this topic in the communication being observed.

Here are the main features of the multidimensional system developed by E. Bayer:

Section 1.   *Functions of communication*

    I.   *Direction of interaction*
1. Teacher to teacher
2. Teacher to class
3. Teacher to part of the class
4. Teacher to one student
5. One student to teacher
6. One student to class
7. One student to part of class
8. One student to one student
9. Class to teacher
10. Class to one student
11. Part of class to teacher
12. Part of class to part of class
13. Part of class to one student

---

[1]For this research, E. Bayer has operationally defined teaching as 'a programmed communication of information'.

II. *Role of interaction*
1. Solicits
2. Responds
3. Reacts to solicitation
4. Reacts to response
5. Comments before solicitation
6. Comments after solicitation
7. Comments before response
8. Comments after response

A. *Communication move*
1. Initiating move (Roles 1 + 3 + 5 + 6)
2. Reflexive move (Roles 2 + 4 + 7 + 8)

B. *Communication type*
1. Interaction (Roles 1 + 2 + 3 + 4)
2. Monologue (Roles 5 + 6 + 7 + 8)

Section 2. *Instructional functions*

I. *Organization*
1. Controls verbal participation of students
2. Controls physical arrangements
3. Controls organization of work
4. Controls student's attention
5. Controls discipline
6. Justifies intervention

II. *Imposition*
1. Imposes information
2. Imposes problems: (a) Closed question
                                  (b) Open question
3. Imposes method of solution or procedure
4. Induces response
5. Responds himself
6. Summarizes, synthesizes

III. *Development*
1. Creates stimulating conditions
2. Accepts and/or clarifies information supplied by student
3. Accepts and/or clarifies procedure freely adopted by student
4. Orients and/or structures students' research
5. Responds to a request for information
6. Summarizes, synthesizes information supplied by students

IV. *Personalization*
1. Personalizes information or problems
2. Invites student to communicate his extra-school experience

    Instructional behaviours (categories II, III, IV)
1. Presentation: (II, 1; II, 2; IV, 1; IV, 2; III, 1; III, 2)
2. Procedure: (11, 3; II, 4; III, 3; III, 4)
3. Production: (II, 5; II, 6; III, 5; III, 6)

    Imposed instruction
1. Presentation: (II, 1; II, 2; IV, 1; IV, 2)
2. Procedure: (II, 3; II, 4)
3. Production: (II, 5; II, 6)

    Developed instruction
1. Presentation: (III, 1; III, 2)
2. Procedure: (III, 3; III, 4)
3. Production: (III, 5; III, 6)

V. *Feedback*
1. Evaluation feedback
    (a) Positive evaluation (unspecified)
    (b) Specific positive evaluation
    (c) Negative evaluation (unspecified)
    (d) Specific negative evaluation

2. Structuring feedback
    (a) Asks for improved response
    (b) Improves response

3. Checking feedback
    (a) Has correctness of response checked
    (b) Checks correctness of response
    (c) Has false response corrected
    (d) Corrects false response

VI. *Affectivity*
1. Positive affectivity
2. Negative affectivity

The most important differences from De Landsheere's system are:

I.   Functions are no longer counted as such; the number of sentences produced by the teacher in the course of a particular function are counted instead. Thus, 40 per cent imposition does not indicate 40 impositive acts out of 100, but that 40 per cent of all sentences pronounced by the teacher were of impositive nature;

II.   The function of concretization has been rejected. De Landsheere himself has suggested that this category was a weakness in his system for reasons of non-exclusiveness;

III.   The category of *feedback* is much broader in Bayer's system, for it covers all verbal reactions of the teacher to the pupil, provided they are related to instruction;

IV. Systematic grouping of categories or sub-categories into instructional behaviour patterns helps to characterize the teaching style;

V. The concepts of imposition and development are modified. Imposition is practically limited to the introduction of information and problems while development relates to the process of problem solving; in this latter case, the teacher supplies information as answers to questions asked by the pupils who are confronted with the problem.

Section 3.   *Cognitive level*

A. *Cognitive level of information*
   1. *Factual information*
   2. *Facts or actions in relation*
   3. *General, abstract information*

B. *Cognitive level of activities*

   (a) Solicited activity
   (b) Effective activity

   I. *Recall*

   II. *Comprehension*
      1. Translates
      2. Interprets
      3. Extrapolates

   III. *Application*
   (The definition of this category is not the same as Bloom's definition. Here it becomes: practice problems and exercises suggested by the teacher for drill.)

   IV. *Analysis*
      1. Elements
      2. Relations

   V. *Synthesis*
      1. Produces personal work
      2. Suggests planned operations

   VI. *Evaluation*
      1. In terms of internal evidence
      2. In terms of external criteria

   Convergent production: (II, 1; II, 2; III)
   Divergent production: (II, 3; IV1; IF, 2; V, 1; V, 2)

For 15 voluntary elementary school teachers, three periods were observed: arithmetic (discussion of a problem), reading (discussion of a text), and science, history or geography.

For each period, three parts were tape-recorded: the first five minutes, from the 15th to the 20th minute, and the last five minutes.

The reliability of coding was checked and was in nearly all cases above 80. However, the reliability coefficient for the cognitive level of activities was mediocre: ·34, ·37, ·49, ·56, ·61.

All data were punched on card and processed by IBM 360 computer. Here are the main results:

I. *Function of communication* . . N = 9,563

    1. *Direction of interaction*
        Teacher to class . . . 36%
        Teacher to one student . . 31·5%
        One student to teacher . . 23%

    2. *Role of interaction*
        Solicits . . . . . 23·5%
        Responds 28%
        Reacts to response . . . 26%
        Comments before solicitation . 6%
        Comments after response . . 9%

      A. *Communication move*
        Initiating 35%
        Reflexive 65%

An average of 15 sentences per minute was observed; this confirms the great role of verbal communication in the instructional process.

Seven times out of 10, the teacher had the initiative in the communication. When the students communicated with the teacher, it was mostly in response to solicitation. Practically no communication from student to students took place (0·6%).

Teacher monologue was low (17·4%) compared with teacher-pupil dialogue (82·6%). This and many other figures obtained by Bayer confirm that communication in the classroom remains strictly under the teacher's control. In this case, each student had less than one opportunity to respond per hour of instruction.

Science instruction proved the most verbal, and arithmetic the least verbal of the three subjects.

The teachers' behaviour was stable; teachers who talked more than others did so in different sections of the period (introduction, middle, end).

A five-minute random sample was representative of the teacher's style of communication, irrespective of the subject taught or of the stage of any period considered. This confirms De Landsheere's observation.

II. *Instructional functions*
   6,792 functions were recorded.

Organization			23%
Imposition . .	40%	⎫	
Development . .	2%	⎬ Instruction	45%
Personalization .	3%	⎭	
Feedback—Evaluation	22%	⎫	
—Structuring	6%	⎬ Feedback	31%
—Checking	3%	⎭	
Affectivity			1%

For all teachers observed in the three subjects (most of whom were considered good teachers by their headmaster or supervisor), the following remarks applied at any time of the period:

Strictly controlled by functions of organization and of feedback, the teacher-student interaction was exclusively geared to instruction (45 per cent), mostly of an impositive nature (40 per cent).

Out-of-school experience of the pupils, and their spontaneous participation, played a very small role. As for affectivity, it hardly had a place in school life.

These observations are characteristic of a strictly subject-matter-centred education and are far from the kind of pedagogy suggested by the Belgian curriculum.

Feedback was mostly of an evaluative nature; furthermore, it was at a low level (91 per cent stereotyped feedback).

Of course, there was a strong relationship between the low level of instruction, marked by a majority of closed factual questions leaving little place for problem solving, and the low level of feedback.

The scarceness of verbalized affective functions (less than one per cent) does not demonstrate a total absence of affective interactions in the classroom. One may think that covert behaviour is here dominant. However, this is only a hypothesis; furthermore, the teacher definitely loses by not using more overt affective reinforcements.

Thus, the analysis of instructional functions confirms the conclusions regarding the structure of communication: teacher-centred education is still predominant.

A five-minute random sample is representative of the whole set of periods.

However, at the individual level, some variations are observed according to the subject matter and stage of the period: the middle of the period fluctuates as far as instructional behaviour is concerned.

The most verbal lessons (science) are also the most impositive.

Cognitive level

1. *Content*

   Factual information   .   .   80%
   Facts or actions in relation   .   19%
   General, abstract information   1%

2. *Activities*

   Recall   .   .   .   41%
   Comprehension   .   42%
   Application   .   .   3%   Convergent   .   40%
   Analysis   .   .   6%   Divergent   .   14%
   Synthesis   .   .   3%
   Evaluation   .   .   5%

No long comments are needed. This teacher-dominated instruction (impositive and convergent) relies mostly on rote learning (41 per cent) and on passive comprehension (42 per cent) of factual information (79 per cent). The immense distance between mythical and real pedagogy could hardly be better illustrated.

Conclusions drawn in the two preceding sections also applied here.

When one looks at all the research results gathered at the Liège Centre, one cannot help being impressed by their cohesion. When the author tackled the problem of classroom interaction analysis some 10 years ago, he thought again and again that something was wrong with the instruments of experiment. Of course, he knew that the situation was not especially bright in our schools: a society has the teachers it deserves; its esteem can be measured at the level of salaries paid. In the present Belgian situation, the elementary school teacher career is chosen by those who are not able to study at college level.

Never had the author imagined, however, that the situation was as desperate as it is. It does not seem exaggerated to say that neither modern educational psychology nor educational theory nor research have had a real impact on school practice.

However weak the present classroom interaction analysis systems may still be, one is more and more convinced that they will play a tremendous role in the improvement of actual school practice by revealing it as it really is, and not as teachers or educationists think or dream it is.

In fact, these analyses are like radiographies: they do not heal the patient but accurately show his state. To use B. Bloom's striking expression, we are losing our innocence in teacher evaluation.

VIII BEYOND VERBAL INTERACTION: THE PRE-SCHOOL LEVEL[1]

In conclusion, we will describe the beginnings of a new method of researching the interactions of the pre-school child. There are not yet any concrete findings from this research, but it is hoped that by making our approach known, we will encourage other work along these lines. The following description is included, then, in the hope that many pre-school child observations using ethological techniques may be undertaken as soon as possible, for only the co-ordinated effort of many scholars will make a real breakthrough possible.

Obviously, not all interactions in the classroom are verbal and, in the primary or secondary school situations thus far described, it is difficult to evaluate what is lost by neglecting non-verbal behaviour.

This issue becomes crucial at kindergarten level. For one thing, the interactions between children seem at least as important as teacher-children interactions. For another, non-verbal behaviour plays a much larger role. A third reason is that verbal communications in a kindergarten setting are often not audible. As a result the design of new types of interaction analysis systems has been undertaken.

An even more difficult problem arises with two-year-old children who are now accepted in what is called pre-kindergarten in Belgium. Here, groups of about 20 two- to three-year-old children are gathered (in many cases for some 10 hours a day) around a teacher or nurse. Nearly all the children come from families with low socio-economic status. We need not insist on the crucial importance for individual and society of this period of life. However, research on interactions at this pre-kindergarten level does not seem to exist to a noticeable extent.

[1]M. Willems-Carels and G. Manni, who are in charge of the 'ethological' project described, are members of the pre-school research team of the *Laboratoire de pédagogie expérimentale* of the University of Liège.

Owing to the psychological characteristics of the two-year-old child, the pre-kindergarten institution cannot be compared with others as far as teacher-'pupil', pupil-pupil or even pupil-physical environment interactions are concerned.

The language of the two-year-old children is still poor: the vocabulary is very limited and the syntactical patterns are just beginning to appear. That is why verbal interactions do not play a great role here: cognitive and affective vehicles of expression and interaction are *actions* and not words: crying, smiling, laughing, shouting, gesturing, manipulating ...

Now, if we define the teacher as 'a mediator between the learner and his environment whose task is to select, create, control and co-ordinate necessary conditions for the learnings desired' (Bayer, 1972), what are the concrete behaviours to be observed in this educational situation (with, in our case, a teacher-pupil ratio of 1/20)?

The teacher cannot rely much on cognitive homogeneity of the group or of any subgroup. How, then, could two-year-old children be guided at the same moment towards the same objective or stimulated to the same course of action? Here, the learning-by-doing principle and the process of individualized education are no longer possible alternatives, but sheer musts.

Another dimension of the problem resides in the 'unnatural' character of the pre-kindergarten environment. Here are toys and furniture specially designed for small children, while the home environment is full of equipment for adults, part of this equipment being manipulated as toys (chairs, tools, etc.). At 'school', divergent use of the material is not so large and the teacher or nurse acts artificially when compared with the home adults. Finally, in most cases, the child personally owns its toys at home, while school equipment and material belong to the community.

Furthermore, one should bear in mind that kindergarten teacher training does not prepare at all for instruction at this age level. Definite official curricula do not exist either.

In order to tackle this new interaction analysis problem, the ethological method has been adopted. A puppet theatre, where the screen is replaced by a one-way mirror, has been installed in rooms where the two- to three-year-olds are. Two observers work together and dictate their observations in a low voice into a tape-recorder. The basic rule is: 'The report should not be in terms of human thought and desires but in terms of observable and activity statements' (Hutt and Hutt, 1970). Moreover, since our aim is the study of interaction between organisms and environment, three aspects are specified (Skinner, 1971):

1. Conditions of response;
2. Response itself;
3. Reinforcing consequences.

Agents of the interactions are:

Teacher-pupil(s);
Pupil-pupil(s);
Teacher-material;
Pupil(s)-material.

Both verbal and motor behaviours are observed.

Motor behaviour raises a special problem, for the observations can be translated in different terms:

(a) In terms of affective or cognitive signification. In this case, words like 'manifestation', 'conflict', 'dependence', 'quest for information' are employed.

(b) In terms of purpose: to play, to manipulate, to search, etc.

(c) In terms of motor components, as happens in all ethological research. This is a necessary stage which, in our opinion, should never be neglected before one proceeds to further analysis and interpretation. In fact, this is the focus of our present research.

Seven periods appearing in a normal day have been selected:

1.	Arrival of the children;	4.	Eating fruit salad;
2.	Free play;	5.	Collective activity;
3.	Preparation of fruit salad by the teacher;	6.	Waiting till mother comes;
		7.	Departure.

Each of the 20 children is observed during five minutes in each of the seven periods. However heavy this approach may seem, it still remains superficial and incomplete. Indeed, time and event sampling sometimes cause a loss of crucial behavioural information, specially at the beginning or conclusion of a sequence. Furthermore, the fact that both observers are in the 'puppet theatre' means that part of the verbal interactions is lost, and so also is some motor behaviour, when children completely turn their back to the mirror.

Our research, as already indicated, is only in its early stages. The furthest we can go now is to describe the method of the first phase of analysis: all motor behaviours observed are analysed in terms of the function of the movement and part of the body concerned. This first ethogram will be progressively refined. All behaviours are also tabulated. Crucial in this approach is that behaviour is not categorized as in usual classroom interaction analysis (for categorizing is already interpreting), but is defined through its relation with other behaviour: the signification of one piece of behaviour is given by the response induced. This relation inventory should help us to understand the educational environment and identify its structuring and destructuring features as far as child development is concerned.

BIBLIOGRAPHY

BAYER, E. (1964). 'Essai d'observation objective du comportement des enseignants.' Unpublished dissertation, University of Liège.

BAYER, E. (1966). 'Etudes objectives des comportements d'enseignement', *Revue Belge de Psychologie et de Pedagogie* (RBPP), **28**, 115, 73–88.

BAYER, E. (1967). 'Comparaison de deux méthodes d'enregistrement des comportements verbaux d'enseignants', *Scientia Paedagogica Experimentalis*, **4**, 1, 98–103.

BAYER, E. (—). 'Quelques hypothèses expérimentales à propos de l'enseignement Decroly', *RBPP*.

BAYER, E. (1972). 'Multidimensional analysis of the verbal communication in the classroom'. Unpublished doctoral dissertation, University of Liège.

DE LANDSHEERE, G. (1963). 'La prédiction et l'évaluation de l'efficacité des professeurs', *RBPP*, **25**, 104, 93–111.

DE LANDSHEERE, G. (1970). *Introduction à la Recherche Pédagogique*. Paris: A. Colin-Bourrelier. Third edition, 163–83.

DE LANDSHEERE, G. (1970). 'La formation des maîtres par l'analyse des interactions pédagogiques'. In: HILLIGEN, W. (Ed.) *Pädagogische Forschung*. Bielefeld: Bertelsman.

DE LANDSHEERE, G. (1971). 'How teachers teach. Analysis of verbal interaction in the classroom', *Classroom Interaction Newsletter*, 7, 1.

DE LANDSHEERE, G. and BAYER, E. (1969). *Comment les maîtres enseignent. Analyse des interactions verbales en classe*. Brussels: Ministere de l'Education nationale, Administration des Etudes. 117.

HUGHES, M. *et al*. (1959). *Development of the Means for the Assessment of the Quality of Teaching in Elementary Schools*. Salt Lake City: University of Utah.

HUTT, S. J. and HUTT, C. (1970). *Direct Observation and Measurement of Behaviour*. Springfield: Charles C. Thomas.

JACQUES, G. (1969). 'L'enseignement de la géographie en première année du secondaire. Analyse des fonctions d'enseignement.' Unpublished dissertation, University of Liège.

MARTIN, J. M. (1970). 'Essai de modification controlée du comportement pédagogique d'un instituteur. Etude des fonctions de feedback'. Unpublished dissertation, University of Liège.

NINANE, A. M. (1969). 'Essai de l'application de la taxonomie de BLOOM (domaine cognitif) a l'analyse des comportements d'enseignement'. Unpublished dissertation, University of Liège.

SKINNER, B. F. (1971). *L'Analyse Experimentale du Comportement*. Translated by RICHELLE. Brussels: Dessart.

VAN CEULEBROECK, M. (1968). 'Approche de 'l'Ecole moderne' (Pédagogie Freinet)'. Unpublished dissertation, University of Liège.

A Study of Student Teachers in the Classroom

E. C. Wragg, BA, MEd, PhD
Department of Education, Exeter University

I. THE RESEARCH CONTEXT

This inquiry, sponsored by the Social Science Research Council, was designed to provide more information about graduate student teachers, about their personalities, their behaviour in the classroom and about factors influencing success and failure.

It was undertaken for a number of reasons. First of all there has been comparatively little research in this country into teacher education. Summaries of research by Evans (1961), Allen (1963), Cane (1968) and Cope (1970) have indicated just over 100 references. Cane (1968), summarizing recent research into teacher training, reported, 'The salary bill for teachers in maintained schools was £450,000,000 in 1963–64—nearly half the total LEA and Ministry educational expenditure. This considerable annual investment in some 300,000 teachers on the staff of maintained schools is backed by astonishingly little information about teacher education, and by few research projects which might be of assistance to those concerned with educating teachers'.

A conference held on July 4th, 1967, and reported by the National Foundation for Educational Research (Cane, 1968), discussed research which might be done in the field of teacher education. The conference report listed a number of areas where research was badly needed. The list was a large one and pointed out by implication the lack of basic research in several vital fields such as teaching practice, attitudes of students, effectiveness of different kinds of teacher training techniques, and use of modern technological aids.

One of the largest gaps in the research literature, as the review of research will show, is created by the absence of any major published study of students on teaching practice in this country using direct observation, and very little using any other technique. There are only a few studies of this kind in existence in the United States, yet the 1963 Yearbook of Education (Bereday and Lauwerys, 1963), which was devoted to the education and training of teachers, shows that a period of teaching practice is a feature of teacher training in almost every country in the world. This present piece of research was intended to provide a descriptive account of the lessons of over 100 student teachers over a $2\frac{1}{2}$-month teaching practice period.

Apart from the need to fill some of the gaps in previous research it was also appropriate that research in teacher education should be conducted at the present time for a variety of reasons.

In 1969 it was announced that teacher training was shortly to be made compulsory, and this announcement highlighted the debate which was already going on over reform in teacher training. National reports on education, even where their main purpose has lain elsewhere, have often commented on teacher training. The McNair Report (1944) proposed two types of school practice, college based and school based with a movement of teaching staff between the two. The Newsom Report (1963) pointed out the need for student teachers to gain sociological insights and to have extra-mural contacts with children, such as camps and youth clubs. The Robbins Report (1963) proposed the BEd degree and Schools of Education. The Plowden Report (1967) solicited the opinions of Heads on teacher training procedures and found that only half felt training was adequate.

Since the Plowden Report pressure for a reform of the education of teachers has come from a number of sources. There have been suggestions that University Departments of Education should no longer train graduates (Pedley, 1969 and NUT, 1970). A Parliamentary select committee heard evidence from all parties concerned, and received a very critical set of evidence from the NFER (Sproule, 1970) about poor preparation for actual teaching, 'obstructionist traditions' in teacher training establishments, over-timetabling and over-lecturing of student teachers and lack of research.

In 1970 the then Minister of Education, Mr Edward Short, asked each Area Training Organization to report on teacher training in its own area. The James Committee, established by Mr Short's successor, Mrs Margaret Thatcher, produced a report (1972) with 133 recommendations, many of which required a substantial restructuring of current practice in teacher education.

The demand for a searching inquiry into teacher training is not confined to this country. In the United States, for example, Koerner (1965) in a powerful attack on teacher training, reports an inquiry at the University of Wisconsin where only 50 per cent of student teachers expressed satisfaction with their education courses. When asked to compare these with other courses they had undergone at University the number expressing satisfaction with education courses fell to 28 per cent.

Stone (1968) visited 48 colleges and universities engaged in teacher training in the United States under the Ford Foundation Breakthrough Program. He observed that

'In an effort to assert academic parity with traditional liberal arts studies, or to adopt a protective coloration for their discipline, Professors of Education in Liberal Arts Colleges relied heavily on the lecture system to present both theoretical and practical material. As a result, students' only opportunity to apply what they had learned was a practice teaching assignment, usually taken in the last half of the senior year, in which they were expected to conform to existing practice, with little or no chance to experiment with new methods and techniques.'

To this must be added the powerful voice of Rogers (1966) and his followers who wish to see a complete overhaul of both teaching, which he calls 'a vastly over-rated function' and teacher training. Rogers argues that for the human race it is a matter of survival that teaching should concern itself with the facilitation of change and learning in a rapidly changing world.

Teacher training, then, is under scrutiny both in Britain and elsewhere, which makes the need for basic research even more critical.

A final reason why basic research is needed is the sheer expansion in numbers of both student teachers and those involved in training them in the last few years. As Morrison and McIntyre (1969) have pointed out, only about 10 per cent of each age group in Britain has had the sort of educational background to become a teacher, but this figure is increasing every year.

Against this background of increasing student numbers, substantial criticism of teacher training procedures, and the absence of any major study of student teachers based on live classroom observation, it was decided that this inquiry should have four main objectives:

(a) to study the classroom behaviour of 100 graduate student teachers.

(b) to relate observed behaviour to measures of personality, values, creativity, intelligence and academic achievement, as well as ratings of effectiveness.

(c) to analyse classroom observation data by subject, sex of class, sex of teacher, type of school and stage of teaching practice at which observations were made.

(d) to explore certain training procedures designed to make the student teacher aware of classroom interaction, and to evaluate their effectiveness in enabling students to modify their behaviour.

II BRIEF REVIEW OF RELEVANT RESEARCH

Since the present inquiry is concerned with the classroom interaction of graduate student teachers there are two major areas of research to consider. First of all there is the research into student teachers and student teaching, and secondly the research into the systematic analysis of classroom interaction.

It was mentioned above that relatively little research has been done in Britain into student teachers and teacher training and that previous reviews by Evans (1961), Allen (1963), Cane (1968) and Cope (1970) had found barely 100 references between them, mainly describing small-scale research. Cope (1970) felt the field was comparatively underdeveloped:

'Material dealing specifically with training establishments in this country, the courses they offer and their professional and social climate is extremely sparse.'

(a) Research into student teachers and their teaching

It is not always possible to isolate research into graduate student teachers as several pieces of research include both non-graduates and graduate in their samples. Obviously there are differences, sometimes significant, between graduates and non-graduate teacher trainees. The University of Toledo (1965) cross-cultural comparison of British and American teacher trainees found the British achievement scores in a number of subject areas very powerfully boosted by the high performance of English and Scottish graduate students. Evans (1964) specifically compared 144 graduates and 145 college students preparing for teaching in the same year on tests of personality and reasoning. He found the graduates scored significantly higher in reasoning ability as measured by Valentine Reasoning Tests, the AH5 and other tests (although 20 per cent of the college students scored on or above the graduate mean scores). On personality tests, however, college students were shown to be significantly more extravert than the graduates.

In addition, research by Ashley, Cohen and Slatter (1967) indicated a greater percentage of middle class students amongst graduates than amongst non-graduate teacher trainees.

A great deal of the research in this field has attempted to secure measures which correlate significantly with ratings of effectiveness. Evans (1952) found no correlation between attitude scores and final teaching mark, or between intelligence scores and final teaching mark when she administered tests to student teachers of four colleges and one department of education. She did find, however, that on her tests, college students registered a more favourable attitude to teaching as a career than the postgraduate students did.

Another study by Evans (1958) examining the Minnesota Teacher Attitude Inventory (MTAI) developed by Cook, Leeds and Callis (1951), a test designed among other things to identify teachers who have good rapport with their pupils, found a correlation between the MTAI scores and theory marks but not teaching practice grades. Cortis (1968) used creativity tests as well as personality tests and related the scores to practical teaching grades, theory marks and academic subject marks in college of education students. He concluded, that 'grades on practical teaching did not correlate significantly with any of the cognitive variables, which may indicate that teaching skill bears no direct relationship to cognitive ability.'

An attempt to discriminate between college students rated as 'good' (A or B teaching mark) and those rated 'poor' (D or E teaching mark) was made by Herbert and Turnbull (1963). They found no significant difference between the two groups on personality variables as measured by personality tests. Their only positive results were for MTAI scores which, they concluded, best separated the two groups.

Mann (1961) used a large battery of tests of personality, intelligence, habits and attitudes, as well as biographical questionnaires and interviews in an attempt to identify the factors influencing success in a teacher training college. His sample of 80 students consisted of 40 men and 40 women spread evenly over the different year groups. He found significant correlations with teaching practice success for a number of variables, including good financial status of family, level and length of education of mother, physical stature and bearing, and, of the personality variables, vitality and dependability.

Warburton, Butcher and Forrest (1963) investigated 118 volunteers out of 133 postgraduate students at Manchester University Department of Education. Final data were assembled for 100 students on 100 variables. An analysis of the correlations between test scores, biographical variables and measures of success such as teaching practice mark showed that the Cattell 16PF scores were amongst the best predictors of success in teaching practice. Conscientiousness, sensitivity and self-control were some of the personality factors showing the highest correlation with teaching practice ratings.

It is important to note at this stage that none of the research quoted used any measures obtained from live observation of student teachers doing their practice. Most were based on scores obtained from attitude or personality tests, or subjective assessment by supervisors.

A major difficulty has been the establishment of satisfactory criterion measures. In most of the research both in Britain and the United States the final teaching mark has been taken as the measure of effectiveness. This is not always an appropriate measure if it is based on the judgment of one supervising tutor, unendorsed by the observations of others.

When she surveyed current methods of assessing teachers' competence, Evans (1951) concluded that the best criterion of effectiveness would be 'a composite measure based on pupil gains in information, ratings by competent observers, and a rating based upon opinions of pupils'.

An American writer, Barr (1961), summarizing a massive amount of American research into teacher effectiveness, pointed out:

'Some teachers were preferred by administrators, some were liked by the pupils, and some taught in classes where there were substantial pupil gains, and generally speaking these were not the same teachers.'

In other words there is comparatively little agreement amongst researchers about one single criterion of good teaching, and studies which have taken pupil gains on achievement tests, and pupil or observer ratings, have produced quite different groups of 'good' teachers.

There is not very good agreement between different observers rating the same teacher, as Barr went on to point out.

'There is plenty of evidence to indicate that different practitioners observing the same teacher teach, or studying data about her, may arrive at very different evaluations of her; this observation is equally true of the evaluation experts; starting with different approaches, and using different data-gathering devices, they, too, arrive at very different evaluations.'

(b) Research into the analysis of classroom interaction

The field of interaction analysis research has expanded rapidly in the last five years in the United States, and is too wide now to be covered fully in a review of this kind. Simon and Boyer (1968 and 1970) have published a 17-volume collection of work which is by no means exhaustive.

A very early piece of work by Stevens (1912) analysed typescripts of lessons and found that teachers talked twice as much as all the children contributed, and asked two to four lower level cognitive questions per minute in every subject. This is surprisingly close to some research findings of recent times, like those of Flanders (1960) and Bellack (1966) described below.

Systematic observation of classroom phenomena really begins in earnest with the work of Anderson (1939) and later Anderson, Brewer and Reed (1945 onwards). Anderson's approach to direct observation was to look for contacts between teachers and children or amongst the children themselves, and divide these into Dominative (use of force, commands, threats, blame, snatching toys etc.) and Integrative (sharing, asking, playing harmoniously, co-operating). The children observed were kindergarten age, and were usually of superior IQ. Anderson used a 23 category system, and two observers watched children for five minutes at a time. His three most important findings were (1) the teacher set the pattern. When teachers were either dominative or integrative, by and large the children followed the pattern. (2) When the teacher's integrative contacts increased the children showed more spontaneity, initiative and greater problem-solving ability. (3) When the teacher's dominative contacts increased the pupils could more easily be distracted from what they were doing.

The famous research by Lewin, Lippitt and White (1939 and 1943) took Anderson's work a stage further and investigated the effects of authoritarian, democratic and laissez-faire leaders in a boys' club setting.

The investigation noted greater aggression amongst the authoritarian groups (40 times as many dominative acts). There was also release of tension when the leader was absent or when they switched from an authoritarian group to a democratic or laissez-faire group. The authoritarian-led groups showed greater dependence on their leader, and were not so likely to work in his absence, whereas the democratic groups did. Afterwards 19 out of the 20 boys in the group said they preferred the democratic style of leadership (the 20th boy was the son of an army officer and liked discipline!). There was also a seven out of ten preference for the laissez-faire style over the authoritarian style.

The next major development is to be found in the work of Withall (1945) who constructed a seven category system for describing the social/emotional climate in classrooms. His system analysed teachers' verbal statements and consisted of three learner-centred categories, three teacher-centred categories, and one neutral category. Four trained judges analysed typescripts of lessons and showed, on average, a 65 per cent agreement with each other. He validated his system against Anderson's categories. He found a consistent teacher pattern from day to day, with the exception of some teachers who had a varied pattern. Withall did not, at that time, however, go on to relate his measures to any other variables.

A later development came from the field of social psychology when Bales and Strodtbeck (1951) developed their 12 category system for analysing tape-recordings of group discussions in an attempt to analyse problem-solving processes. They drew conclusions about which type of behaviour was likely to occur at various stages of solving a problem in a group. It was largely from the work of Bales and Withall that Flanders developed his own system.

Flanders (1951) measured galvanic skin response and heartbeat rate of children exposed to dominative and integrative role playing teachers. He found that under a dominative pattern children showed greater anxiety and were less able to recall the material studied, which supported Anderson's findings. Under primarily integrative teaching the opposite effect was noted.

Later Flanders (1963) developed a ten category system for analysing verbal interaction in the classroom. The system is described in detail below and is the one used in this present research. Briefly the categories consisted of seven for teacher talk, two for pupil talk and one for silence or confusion. Of the seven teacher talk categories, four represented what Flanders called 'indirect influence', i.e. praise, accepting ideas or feelings, asking questions, and three were what he called 'direct' influence, i.e. lecturing, giving commands or criticising. Flanders' use of 'indirect' and 'direct' is closely related to Anderson's 'dominative' and 'integrative' concepts.

As the volume of work reporting live observations of teachers has grown, so too has the number using systematic analysis techniques. Cogan (1958) already had a large number of references in his summary of research into teacher-pupil interaction, and by 1968 Simon and Boyer reported 26 different classroom observation instruments in regular use in a six volume survey. Two years later the same two writers (Simon and Boyer 1970) produced another eleven volumes in which they had collected articles describing 92 systems of interaction analysis most of which were being used in classrooms. These included systems for verbal and non-verbal analysis; systems that had affective or cognitive categories, or both; systems for analysing science lessons or modern language lessons; systems using video-tape or sound tape recording techniques, using one live observer or two, for elementary or secondary—a very wide range. Some of the systems took a sample every three or five seconds, some recorded continuously for one whole minute, some concentrated on the teacher only, a single child, or both teacher and class.

Although British research into classroom interaction behaviour patterns has increased in recent years, there is still little published about trainee teachers. A number of American investigators have studied student teachers in the classroom.

Schueler, Gold and Mitzel (1962) analysed filmed records of 54 student teachers taken at the beginning and end of their teaching practice. They noted at the end of the practice more information in what the teacher said, greater class order and greater awareness by the teachers of children's difficulties. There was some variation according to the type of class being taught.

Kirk (1964) trained a group of student teachers preparing to teach in elementary schools in the Flanders system and then observed this group and a matched but untrained group on teaching practice. He found that, for all students taken as a single group, the amount of teacher talk declined over the teaching practice period. The experimental group, however, elicited more spontaneous children's contributions, engaged in more open discussions and spent less time in continuous lecture. Kirk denies having pointed the experimental group in any particular direction when training them, but admits having made them aware of previous research findings. Presumably this would effectively point them in the direction of greater indirectness and persuade them to elicit more child talk.

Zahn (1965) took 92 student teachers preparing to teach in elementary schools and gave training in the Flanders system to one quarter of them (n=23) chosen at random. The group which had been trained showed more positive attitudes to teaching after teaching practice on a pencil and paper test than the others. He also used the Scale of Dogmatism developed by Rokeach (1960) to measure degree of openness or closedness of mind. He found that the more open-minded on this test were more likely to be rated proficient on teaching practice, irrespective of whether they were trained in interaction analysis or not. There was also some evidence that, for students at the more closed-minded end of the scale, interaction analysis training had an impact on changing their attitudes to more positive ones as measured by the attitude test, possibly because of the structure it offered. There was no evidence that the trained group was rated more highly than the rest on teaching practice.

Furst (1967b) took matched groups of student teachers preparing to teach in secondary schools. She gave one group training in interaction analysis *before* teaching practice, one group training *during* teaching practice, and a third parallel group no training at all. She found that the trained groups showed more acceptance of children's ideas and less rejection of their ideas than the untrained group. She also found that those trained *during* teaching practice produced more children's talk.

Moskowitz (1967) reported an experiment where the supervising teachers in the teaching practice schools were included. She took 44 student teachers and the 44 co-operating teachers who were to supervise their teaching practice. She arranged them at random into four groups. Group one was for students and teachers who were both going to be trained to use the Flanders system, group two would have students trained but the teachers untrained, group three would be for the teachers trained but not the students, and group four would have students and teachers both untrained. She administered questionnaires to all 88 participants to measure the positiveness of their attitudes to each other. She also recorded observations of all 88 of them in their classrooms. She concluded that attitudes were most positive to each other in group one, where both had been trained in the system. In group two she detected least positive attitudes of students to co-operating teachers (this was the group which had students trained but teachers untrained). Groups one and two (students trained) showed significantly more indirect teaching than groups three and four (students untrained).

Gunnison (1968) took 10 student teachers whose teaching style had been observed, using Flanders' technique, to be primarily direct. Half the sample, randomly selected, was given a six-hour course in interaction analysis. The control group received no such instruction. Subsequent observation of all the group showed significantly increased extended indirect influence by the experimental group and significantly greater amounts of pupil talk in the same group. The experimental group was also rated higher by the children. As in many other similar pieces of research there is no control for Hawthorn effect in this experiment. The sample is also too small for very much significance to be inferred from the findings. In addition, analysis of Gunnison's data shows a significant rise in the i/d ratio[1] of the *control* group which she does not explain.

Almost all this research has tended to concern itself with the effects of certain types of training rather than describe the teaching behaviour of the students.

Descriptive studies of the classroom behaviour of experienced teachers in the United States have often shown quite a high agreement with each other on certain aspects of classroom interaction.

When Flanders (1963) summarized early research in interaction analysis, he looked at data on 147 teachers from all grade levels. At this time he formulated his 'rule of two-thirds', which was that two-thirds of the lessons observed was talk, two-thirds of this talk was by the teacher, and two-thirds of what the teacher said was in the form of a lecture. For teachers rated 'poor' he had found a rule of three-quarters was more the norm.

Bellack *et al.* (1966) analysed tapes of social studies lessons. By allocating 'lines' of typescript to teacher or pupils they found 72 per cent belonged to the teacher. In addition an analysis of 'moves', such as initiating interaction, soliciting responses, reacting to what has been said etc., showed that 82 per cent of these were initiated by the teacher.

A number of American studies have related observed classroom behaviour to various criterion measures. Sometimes these have been ratings of effectiveness by administrators or other people.

Amidon and Giammatteo (1965) investigated a total of 153 elementary school teachers in 11 school districts of Pennsylvania. Each of the eleven districts was asked to identify three teachers they regarded as 'superior' to enable the investigators to compare the verbal interaction patterns of these 33 'master' teachers with the other 120. The Flanders system was used as an observation instrument. The 'superior' teachers showed significantly more acceptance of children's ideas, less criticism, and encouraged significantly more child-initiated talk than did the other teachers.

Amidon and Giammatteo's findings had been supported to some extent by earlier work reported by Flanders (1962) who in 1956/57 had conducted a cross-cultural study comparing classrooms in the USA with those in New Zealand. He used a paper and pencil test with a large sample of over 1,000 pupils in each of these countries to assess pupils' perceptions of 'teacher attractiveness', 'fair rewards and punishments', 'independence of teacher supervision' etc. He then used his own system to collect data from live classroom observations on those teachers scoring very high or very low.

In both the USA and New Zealand the teacher scoring high on the pupil attitude inventory tended to be more indirect and to allow more pupil participation.

Other criterion measures have included pupil achievement. Powell (1968) visited a large number of schools where the teaching staff had been relatively stable for a number of years. He was able, by using the Flanders system for observing in these schools, to find classes of children at the elementary school level who had been exposed to three successive years of primarily direct or indirect teaching. Analysis of the achievement scores of these

---

[1]A measure of teacher 'indirectness' proposed by Flanders (1965). It is a ratio of some of his 'indirect' categories such as praise and acceptance of ideas and feelings, and 'direct' ones such as command and criticism.

classes showed no difference in reading scores, but the classes who had had three years of indirect teaching scored significantly higher on arithmetic tests and on a composite of all test scores combined.

Furst (1967) took a sample of 345 children in seven New York High Schools which had been used in the research reported by Bellack *et al.* (1966). Fifteen teachers taught specially prepared material to matched classes. Comparison of before and after achievement tests showed that three teachers produced high gains, eight average and four low gains. When Furst used Flanders' technique to analyse tapes of the lessons she found that the 'high' group of teachers was more indirect, used less teacher talk, more silence, and gave more directions in the later stages of the units. The 'low' group was more direct and gave more directions on the first day of the units.

Rosenshine (1969) summarized research into interaction analysis data which had been related to pupil achievement. He found that teacher approval in some form was usually associated with higher achievement and criticism was usually associated with lower achievement. He quoted two studies which found the reverse. Perkins (1965) discovered a relationship between rejecting children's answers and higher achievement in arithmetic, and Spaulding (1965) found greater gains in reading under teachers who commanded conformance and elicited clarification in a non-threatening way.

This brief review of some of the research in the fields of student teachers and classroom behaviour has revealed certain important needs. Much of the work on interaction analysis has been done in the United States, largely with experienced teachers. Some of the evidence has suggested that certain types of behaviour by the teacher are significantly associated with measures of effectiveness such as ratings by children or supervisors or with pupil gains.

Since no British study had examined the classroom behaviour of a sizeable group of teacher trainees, it seemed important that such a study should be undertaken, using appropriate descriptive techniques. The present research was designed to meet these requirements and provide information not previously available.

III DESIGN OF THE RESEARCH

(a) Definition of terms and theoretical model

Throughout this account the terms *presage*, *process* and *product* variables will be used in the sense in which many American writers use the terms (Flanders and Simon, 1969), when writing about research in teaching. *Presage* variables are those which exist in the situation *before* manipulation, or at the beginning of the research, and would include scores such as IQ, attitude measures, personality test scores of either teachers or children or both. *Process* variables are those which are measured during the *actual teaching*, and include any indications of classroom behaviour, verbal or non-verbal, equipment used etc. *Product* variables are the *results* of what happens in classrooms and would involve gains or losses on achievement tests, attitude change shown by teachers or children, and ratings of effectiveness of teachers by pupils or supervisors.

The theoretical model on which the research is based assumes that there is a constant flow of influence across the three types of variable in both directions. *Presage variables* such as the teacher's personality or a child's IQ can influence the classroom *process*, sometimes significantly. Warm, accepting teachers may be more likely to listen to children talking, accept their ideas and feelings. Bright children may initiate a great deal more than duller children. Turner (1967) discovered that the teachers found to be more indirect in Flanders' 1960 study had had brighter children in their classes. Both *presage* and *process variables* can influence the *products* of teaching either separately or together. Bright children might learn despite the teacher or because of her. Physically attractive teachers might be rated more highly despite their classroom performance, or their attractiveness might enhance their rapport with children and hence their rating.

The influence is also to be detected in the reverse direction. The *product variables* will affect future *processes*. For example, teachers of children learning effectively may be reinforced to continue teaching along similar lines, and teachers suspecting unfavourable attitudes or learning developing may feel they must change their teaching. The influence can go back to the *presage variables*, in that on future occasions they will be different as a result of time and experience. A measure of children's values, for example, made before research began would be a *presage variable*. If classroom *processes* changed children's values then the extent and direction of change would be a *product variable*. On a future occasion, however, a second piece of research would record the new changed value structure as *presage variables*. A simplified theoretical model showing some of the variables in each category and high-lighting the ones measured in the present research is given below.

The review of research showed that a number of questions about student teachers remained unanswered in the literature. At the graduate level, for example, where students were preparing to teach in secondary schools, what were the differences amongst teachers

Presage variables	*Process variables*	*Product variables*
Children:	*Children:*	*Children:*
Physical attributes;	*verbal interaction:*	Amount and nature of
social and family	**with teacher;	learning achieved;
background;	(**) with pupils;	attitude change.
experience in school;	*non-verbal interaction:*	
personality;	with teacher;	
values;	with pupils;	
cognitive skills—	with equipment, etc.;	
IQ; creativity, etc.;	movement;	
*attitudes.	thought processes.	
Teachers:	*Teachers:*	*Teachers:*
Physical attributes;	*verbal interaction:*	Amount and nature of
social and family	**with class;	children's learning
background;	(**) with individuals;	induced;
experience in school;	*non-verbal interaction:*	*Amount and nature of
**personality;	with class;	teacher's learning
**values;	with individuals;	(including feedback
cognitive skills—	with equipment;	about own behaviour);
**IQ;	movement;	**Ratings of competence.
**creativity;	thought processes.	
attitudes;		
**academic achievement.		

Simplified Theoretical Model
  ** Indicates variables measured in the present research.
(**) Sometimes recorded.
  * Pilot phase only.

of different subjects? Were there differences in classroom behaviour between men and women, or between classes in single sex schools and mixed schools? Were there differences according to type of school—Secondary Modern, Grammar or Comprehensive? Did patterns change as teaching practice progressed? Were there different patterns in classes containing younger or older children?

In addition, because of the lack of descriptive material about the classrooms of student teachers there was obviously going to be no research describing the effect of presage variables on process variables. What influenced different patterns of classroom behaviour? Was it a student's personality, his values, his intelligence or academic achievement? Were 'creative' teachers very flexible and less 'creative' teachers very rigid in their approach?

Nor was there any evidence about possible links between process and product variables. The absence of live observation data left a number of questions in this area unanswered. What effect did various kinds of classroom behaviour by the teacher have on children's attitudes? What effect did it have on the ratings of effectiveness given to students by schools and supervisors? Did they tend to favour some types of classroom behaviour and not others? Were there any common characteristics in the observed behaviour of those students rated as 'good'? Similarly was there a recognisable pattern or series of patterns amongst student teachers rated as 'poor'?

Furthermore there were no known 'norms' against which innovations in teacher training pocedures could be matched. Colleges and departments of education seeking to change their training procedures have no published data about classroom behaviour with which to compare their own students. Consequently the measures and procedures in the present research were chosen to provide information as partial answers to some of the general and specific questions outlined above.

(b) Measuring the presage variables

A great deal of thought preceded the final choice of the 28 presage variables and the procedures for attempting to measure them. The presage variables were intended here to serve two purposes. They were to be related to both the process variables and the product variables.

Consequently what was needed was the maximum amount of useful information which could be collected from students as a group at the beginning of the session. For this and other reasons a number of approaches were rejected. A lengthy series of successive testing sessions was rejected because it would (a) postpone or interfere with the beginning of the course and (b) quite possibly lose the goodwill of a number of students who might come to resent being scrutinized and subjected to testing sessions so shortly after many of them are relieved to have finished with finals. Previous research (Wragg, 1967) suggested that students often begin their training year with a number of expectations. They hope, for example, that the year will be different from what they have experienced previously, and that they will broaden what they regard as a previously narrow education. Lengthy testing sessions might needlessly antagonize them.

Attitude tests like the MTAI were rejected because of the reservations about their appropriateness expressed by Evans (1966) and others. Regular testing and interviewing in the Michaelmas term was also rejected because there would be sufficient scrutiny of the eventual sample once they were engaged in teaching practice.

Finally it was decided to administer four carefully chosen tests on the first day of the Michaelmas Term to all students in the Department. The tests were (a) Cattell's 16PF test form C for variables 1 to 16, (b) The Allport, Vernon, Lindzey 'Study of Values' (Richardson's British form) for variables 17 to 22, (c) The Torrance tests of Creative Thinking (Verbal Test) for variables 23 to 26, (d) The Alice Heim AH5 Group test of high grade intelligence for variable 27. (Variable 28 was to be the student's class of degree taken from his record card.)

All of these tests have been used with teachers or trainee teachers. The Cattell 16PF test 'tests as much of the total personality as can be covered by questionnaire, according to the most up-to-date psychological research'[1] Its advantage is that it provides scores of 16 personality variables and can be completed in around 30 minutes. The 16 factors identified are the results of extensive factor analysis by the test author.[2]

Getzels and Jackson (1963) report three more pieces of research using the Cattell 16PF with teachers. Erickson (1954) found significant correlations between high G (conscientious) low M (conventional), low O (confident) and high Q3 (self-controlled) and various measures of teacher effectiveness.

Hadley (1954) looked at student teachers rated above average or below average and found the 'good' group to be significantly lower on factor F and higher on Factor G than the 'poor' group. This contradicts Lamke's (1951) findings on Factor F as does his other evidence that the 'good' group was low on Factor N (simple, naive).

Only one piece of research relating the 16PF test to process variables has been found by the writer. Flanders and Simon (1969) quote a piece of research by Davies (1961) which found a small positive correlation between Cattell's Factor A (warmth) and responsive teacher behaviour as calculated from Flanders' interaction data obtained from 51 Junior High School teachers.

The 16PF test is open to criticism in that the test-retest correlations for form C are little low for certain factors. Nevertheless it is still a powerful heuristic tool for the investigator studying teachers' personality.

Richardson's British form of the Allport-Vernon-Lindzey Study of Values was used with postgraduate students by Evans (1967). She found no significant change in scores obtained from the sample at the beginning and end of the year.

Getzels and Jackson report two pieces of research using the original American version of the test. Seagoe (1946) gave the test to student teachers and then correlated the scores with teaching practice ratings two years later and principals' ratings four years later. She found a small correlation between low scores on 'economic' and teaching practice grade, and another small correlation between high scores on 'aesthetic' and principals' ratings.

Tanner (1954) studied 44 'superior' student teachers and 22 'inferior' student teachers as revealed by teaching practice ratings and MTAI scores. There were some significant differences. The 'superior' group of women were significantly lower on economic and higher on social values than the 'inferior' women.

The Study of Values is by no means a perfect test. It can be criticised for producing measures only for desirable values rather than base ones such as expediency or hedonism, and the ipsative[3] nature of the data produced means that caution must be exercised in

---

[1]CATTELL, R. B. (1962). *Handbook Supplement for Form C of the Sixteen Personality Factor Questionnaire.* Institute for Personality and Ability Testing, Champaign, Illinois. Page 5.

[2]For a much fuller recent account of the rationale, statistical concepts and procedures, and explanation of personality testing, see CATTELL, R. B. (1970). *The Scientific Analysis of Personality*, especially Chapters 2, 3, 4 and 5. Pelican, London.

[3]A high score on some values automatically means a low score on others.

correlational studies. Richardson has, however, produced a test with Kuder-Richardson reliability coefficients ranging from 0·78 to 0·95, and has shown that scores on the test correspond closely with personal estimates of the values made by the respondents. The political value appears to have less validity on this criterion than the other five values.

The Torrance Tests of Creative Thinking (Verbal Test Form B) which were used as measures of verbal creativity produce three scores for fluency, flexibility and originality, as well as a total score.

Torrance (1966) reports little research into the classroom behaviour of creative or non-creative teachers. Torrance and Hansen (1965) studied the classroom behaviour of six highly creative and six of the least creative teachers in a large metropolitan area. The high scoring teachers asked significantly more divergent questions and significantly fewer questions which merely required reproduction of textbook information than the low scoring teachers.

Webb (1968) found a positive relationship between the creativity scores of classes of children and indirect teaching style as measured by the Flanders system.

The question of the validity of the Torrance tests has not been entirely resolved, and the method of scoring for originality, based on responses of a relatively small American sample, is not wholly satisfactory. However it was decided that verbal fluency could be an important factor in student teachers' verbal classroom behaviour and that the tests might at least give some indications of ways in which future research might be refined.

The final test in the battery was the AH5 Test of high-grade intelligence which has been shown by Heim (1968) to distinguish between Oxford students gaining good and poor degrees in PPP finals. This test, the students' class of degree and the four Torrance creativity scores give six measures of high cognitive ability. Getzels and Jackson (1963),[1] reviewing American research conclude that the relationship between high intellectual skills and the teacher's behaviour and effectiveness have not yet been fully explored. Lack of positive results may be due to a number of factors. Firstly the tests used were normally the traditional IQ tests. The tests used here are both IQ and Creativity tests. Secondly the IQ tests used by most researchers are the normal ones designed for the population at large, whereas this research used the AH5 a 'high-grade' intelligence test. Thirdly, most research has merely looked for links between cognitive abilities as measured by a narrow range of tests and ratings of teaching ability. This research uses a wider range of tests and relates the scores both to ratings of teaching ability and measures of classroom behaviour, which should provide a great deal more information on the effect of higher cognitive ability on these two sets of variables.

(c) **Measuring the process variables**

What goes on in the classroom can be measured or described in a number of different ways. Live observation of lessons has the disadvantage of making it likely that the lesson may be altered in some way by the presence of an outside observer. Flanders (1970) reports an inquiry by Samph who studied the effects on teachers' behaviour of the presence of an observer in the classroom. By monitoring tapes of the lessons, Samph was able to see what the differences were when observers appeared. Using the Flanders system for analysing the observation data he found some tendency to become more oriented towards the children when an observer was present as shown by increases in the categories describing acceptance of children's ideas and questioning. This research was based on a small sample

[1] In GAGE, N. L. (1963) op. cit., p. 574.

of only ten teachers, but it does provide tentative evidence that teachers are likely to make some changes in their behaviour when outsiders are present.

The advantages of a live observer are numerous. He can focus on particular aspects of lessons, his perceptions are first-hand, and he can record as he observes. The Flanders system used in this research requires one observer who concentrates on verbal behaviour: what is said by teachers and children. It divides talk into ten categories, seven for talk by the teacher, two for talk by the children, and a tenth category for non-talk such as silence, or for periods when nothing can be coded at all. The ten categories, with Flanders' own description of them, are given below.

The Flanders System—The Ten Categories

Indirect influence	1.	Accepts feeling: accepts and clarifies the feeling tone of the students in a non-threatening manner. Feelings may be positive or negative. Predicting and recalling feelings are included.
	2.	Praises or encourages: praises or encourages student action or behaviour. Jokes that release tension, not at the expense of another individual, nodding head or saying 'uh huh?' or 'go on' are included.
	3.	Accepts or uses ideas of student: clarifying, building, or developing ideas or suggestions by a student. As teacher brings more of his own ideas into play, shift to category five.
	4.	Asks questions: asking a question about content or procedure with the intent that a student answer.

Teacher talk

Direct influence	5.	Lectures: giving facts or opinions about content or procedure; expressing his own ideas; asking rhetorical questions.
	6.	Gives directions: directions, commands, or orders with which a student is expected to comply.
	7.	Criticizes or justifies authority: statements intended to change student behaviour from non-acceptable to acceptable pattern; bawling someone out; stating why the teacher is doing what he is doing; extreme self-reference.

Student talk	8.	Student talk-responses: talk by students in response to teacher. Teacher initiates the contact or solicits student statement.
	9.	Student talk-initiation: talk by students, which they initiate. If 'calling on' student is only to indicate who may talk next, observer must decide whether student wanted to talk. If he did, use this category.

	10.	Silence or confusion, pauses, short periods of silence, and periods of confusion in which communication cannot be understood by the observer.

Simon and Boyer (1970) describe 92 interaction analysis systems, 79 of which concentrate on verbal behaviour in classrooms. Of these the majority, 56 look at both the teacher and the pupils, 15 look at the teacher only, and 8 look at pupils' verbal behaviour only.

On the negative side the Flanders system could be said to have ideological components in that it looks specifically for 'indirect' teacher talk (with which it would be easy to associate value terms such as 'progressive', 'child-centred', 'democratic') and 'direct' teaching (with its associations of 'authoritarianism', 'telling', 'learning-centred'). Flanders has always stressed, however, that he is not positing a single model of 'good' teaching or recommending teachers to follow any one type of behaviour. Nevertheless it would be wrong to deny that many of the research findings point in the direction of indirect teaching being associated with various measures of effectiveness as the review of research showed.

Another criticism one could make is that the system fails to subdivide important categories like two (praise), into 'cursory praises' and 'sincere praise', or category four (questions) into 'narrow questions' i.e. those which require a short response, usually self-evident, and 'broad questions' which require a longer answer or offer a wider area of possible response. Amidon and Hunter (1966) have made this latter subdivision. Category 10 can be said to be too broad, and to fail to make the distinction made by Hough (1966) in his 16 category system between (a) directed practice or activity, i.e., non-verbal behaviour resulting from the teacher setting the children to work, (b) silence, (c) demonstration, e.g. the teacher showing visual materials or writing on the board, and (d) irrelevant behaviour such as high noise level or confusion.

One can also point out that the Flanders system fails to identify the individual child responding, though the present writer has developed a system for doing this (Wragg 1970 d); and that it is difficult to use in informal settings, and presupposes that the teacher is going to give what some American writers call 'a recitation lesson', though the present writer has adapted it to informal settings (Evans and Wragg, 1969). It is heavily biased towards the cognitive side and has little on the affective side, though one must not forget category one and elements of two and three.

On the positive side the system has a great deal to recommend it as a research tool. The 10 categories make for easy processing. Training observers, a problem discussed below, is, on the whole, straightforward. The information provided is comprehensive within the limitations mentioned above, and ten categories are very much less cumbersome than the vast numbers of categories employed by some investigators, such as Adams and Biddle (1970) with 87 different categories. In addition it has extra uses as a feedback tool in that the data can easily be put in a comprehensible form for teacher trainees or experienced teachers, and it is less value-laden than some systems, despite the points made above. Certain systems, like that of Hough (1966) with teacher categories such as 'corrective feedback' are clearly, as the system author admits, wedded to behaviourist learning theory.

Given the reservations expressed above about the problems of direct observation of classroom phenomena, of the numerous observations system published in research journals the Flanders system seemed the most compact, providing the greatest amount of useful information which could be collected by trained observers without either putting too great a strain on them, or intruding too much in the lessons being observed.

Flanders (1970) describes a number of ratios which can be calculated from matrices assembled from raw data. In the present research each student was observed for between four and six lessons, producing between 2,400 and 3,600 raw tallies. Several matrices can be summed and reduced to a base of 1,000, called a millage matrix, thus making the data comparable between one teacher and another. A total of 22 process variables were extracted from the students' millage matrices and a 23rd variable computed from the matrices on their first four lessons. Details of these process variables are given in the appendix.

(d) Measuring the product variables

In the foregoing review of research the difficulty of rating teacher effectiveness was discussed; it was decided in the present research to use three measures of competence.

The first was the rating by the Head and supervising teachers in the teaching practice school. Following a procedure suggested by Wiseman (1963), a team of four judges experienced in the assessment of student teachers read school reports independently and interpreted them as ratings of effectiveness on the commonly used A-E scale. Product moment correlations for inter-observer agreement were very high, ranging from $+\cdot91$ to $+\cdot94$. The four ratings were summed and the mean calculated.

The second measure of effectiveness was a rating by the supervising tutor, again using the A-E scale. Since both the tutor and the school ratings are subjective a third measure, the composite of the two scores, was used as a consensus of 'those competent to judge'.

(e) The execution of the research

In the pilot study during the 1968/69 year observations were made during approximately 100 lessons given by 31 students. Computer programs were written for high speed processing of Flanders matrices on the Exeter University computer, and certain alterations made to the original plans. A new lesson observation sheet was designed, as were pocket timers to signal a three-second interval to the observer collecting interaction data.

For the main study in 1969/70 all 153 entrants to the Exeter University Department of Education were given the test battery on the first day of the Michaelmas Term in October 1969. All the tests were scored according to procedures described in the test handbook. The two scorers of the Torrance tests showed correlations with each other of $+\cdot99$ for fluency, $+\cdot87$ for flexibility and $+\cdot86$ for originality.

In November 1969 videotapes and sound tapes were prepared for training observers and for reliability checks. All materials were assembled and pocket timers were made and tested. Heads of schools received letters asking for co-operation should their school be in the sample of students being watched. No head refused; many showed considerable interest when observers later travelled around the schools.

In December 1969 five observers were recruited and trained, using sound tapes, videotapes and live lessons. Inter-observer agreements, calculated by a formula suggested by Scott (1955), were high. Flanders suggests that reliability coefficients should be given as comparisons with another trained observer when one is training new observers, the other trained observer usually being the investigator himself. On the final reliability check based on a 30-minute live lesson the five observers obtained Scott coefficients of 0·83, 0·84, 0·86, 0·86 and 0·90 with the present writer.

After two weeks out in schools all the observers met once more for a conference and further reliability check. Scott coefficients on this occasion based on a 20-minute sound tape of a lesson were 0·85, 0·86, 0·87, 0·89 and 0·89 with the present writer.

At the end of the whole project a final reliability check was made and on a 15-minute sound tape the five observers obtained Scott coefficients of 0·85, 0·85, 0·87, 0·87 and 0·91 with the present writer. A check for *intra*-observer reliability was also made at the same time on a 15-minute sound tape which had been coded by the observers two months previously. Intra-observer reliability for all six people, including the present writer who had also been collecting data, was 0·86, 0·88, 0·88, 0·89, 0·91 and 0·92. Intra-observer reliability is the amount by which an observer agrees with his former coding of the same sound tape.

A sample of 104 students was chosen on the basis of geographical location and what each observer could be expected to cover in one term. Of the original sample of 104 one student left the course and so could not be observed, and one other student changed schools midway through the term and was also ill, so he was dropped too, giving a final sample of 102 students.

The 102 students consisted of 56 men and 46 women teaching in 41 different schools in the South-west of England.

Once the observers had been trained to a high level of inter-observer reliability and the 102 students to be observed had been chosen, the next stage was to plan the observation schedules for each individual observer. Since the 23 process variables were eventually going to be calculated from the observation data, and since an analysis of all the data was going to be performed by age of children, type of school, stage of the teaching practice term and so on, it was important that each student should be observed for a 'representative' set of lessons.

Clearly there would be no point in attempting to compare one student who had been watched six times teaching a first form in January with another student who had been observed teaching only a double period with a small sixth form in March. Considerable time was spent determining what would be an acceptable 'representative' sample of a student's teaching practice, in consultation with Dr Paul Kline of the Exeter University Psychology Department.

Flanders suggests six lessons as constituting a usable sample, though many published researches have used two or even a single lesson, and few have in fact used as many as six. It was decided that the target would be six lessons, and that no student would be included in the sample if he had been observed for less than four. Since all the data were eventually to be converted to millage matrices[1] for each student, the differences between students who had been watched for four, five or six lessons would be minimized. In practice this target was 94 per cent realized. Out of a maximum possible 612 lessons 578 were actually observed. Seventy-eight students were watched for six lessons, 14 for five lessons and 10 for four lessons.

Another important point was that the lessons should be spaced. Observers were told to arrange the term in three periods, roughly equal to a beginning, middle and end period, and see that each student was visited in each of these periods. Similarly observers were told to see each student with a spread of classes representing what he had on his timetable, so that lower school (first and second year), middle school (third, fourth year) and upper school (fifth, sixth year) lessons would be included. Obviously some students would not teach a fifth or sixth year class, and others might not teach a first or second year, but observers were to use their judgment. Visits were reported to the present writer weekly, and duplicated visiting schedules were maintained as a check in case any observer was not spreading visits evenly. This check was carried out carefully, but all observers covered the students very successfully.

The observers not only collected Flanders interaction data on each lesson; they also wrote an account of the lesson on the back of the data sheet shortly afterwards, usually the same day. This meant that there were also 578 detailed accounts of the lessons in addition to the interaction data. They also wrote a separate account of any lesson which seemed to need a special report for any reason, and a summary report of their experiences at the end of the whole project. These accounts of the lesson were necessary (a) to amplify the interaction data by giving a fuller picture of what happened in the lesson, and (b) to enable the present

[1] A millage matrix is used to enable rough comparisons to be made between large raw matrices. All tallies in the large matrices are reduced to a base of 1,000. The process is similar to the use of percentages.

writer to give explanations in behavioural terms to certain patterns observed in different subjects, different schools etc.

After teaching practice was concluded, school and tutor reports were collected and a correlation of +·648 between the two sets of scores was obtained. This is close to the correlation of +·60 obtained in similar circumstances by Poppleton (1968), and probably reflects close co-operation between tutors and schools rather than a totally separate evaluation by the two groups.

Finally, the 578 lesson matrices were computed on the University computer and subjected to the data processing described below.

IV THE RESULTS OF THE RESEARCH[1]

(a) Analysis by group and stage of teaching practice

Matrix interpretation has been discussed by Flanders (1970). A simple flow chart can be drawn over a full matrix showing important transitions from cell to cell. Matrix interpretation plays an important part in interaction analysis research, and it should not be undertaken separately from some written accounts by observers of the lessons watched, otherwise the attempted analysis of flow in a lesson or group of lessons becomes too speculative.

In addition to the percentages of talk and teacher talk, ten other ratios are given with each matrix. All are described fully by Flanders (1970), but are summarized briefly here.

I/D ratio: A measure of teacher 'indirectness' which compares categories one, two, three and four with five, six and seven.

i/d ratio: Another measure of teacher 'indirectness' which Flanders claims is less dependent on content than the I/D ratio because it ignores categories four and five (question and lecture) and compares categories one, two and three with six and seven.

Teacher response ratio (TRR): Like the remaining ratios lies between 0 and 100. It measures the teacher's tendency to respond with praise or acceptance to children's answers.

Teacher question ratio (TQR): Measures the teacher's tendency to use question rather than lecture in the more content-oriented parts of the lesson.

Pupil initiation ratio (PIR): Shows how much of the children's talk was initiated by them rather than by the teacher.

Instantaneous teacher response ratio (TRR8/9): Measures the teacher's tendency to integrate children's ideas into class discussion as soon as they have stopped talking.

Instantaneous teacher question ratio (TQR 8/9): similar to the ratio above in that it measures the teacher's tendency, immediately children have stopped talking, to ask a question rather than begin lecturing.

[1]A full account of the results of the research is to be found in WRAGG (1972).

Content cross ratio (CCR): A high score usually indicates greater concern with subject matter with the teacher playing a very active part.

Steady state ratio (SSR): A high score indicates that talk tends to stay in the same category, whereas a low score is produced in lessons where there is rapid interchange between teacher and pupils.

Pupil steady state ratio (PSSR): Measures the extent to which children sustain their contributions to classroom dialogue. Teachers who interrupt the flow of children's talk produce lower scores than these who do not.

The abbreviated forms, TRR, TQR, etc., are given below the matrices.

(a) *The whole group*

Amidon and Flanders (1963) and Flanders (1970) have produced the nearest approximation to 'norms' of classroom behaviour based on observations of lessons using the Flanders system. Since these are calculated entirely from American observations of experienced teachers, mainly in Maths, English and Social Studies, and largely at 6th to 8th grade level, they are of limited use and serve only as a means of comparison. The American 'norms' are approximate and are not meant by their proposers to be authoritative.

Table 1 shows the millage matrix computed for all 578 lessons in the sample and represents a reduction from 337,617 raw tallies.

To summarize the data for the whole group it seems as if comparison with reported American data shows the British student teacher group as a whole to be less likely to accept ideas and feelings, but also less likely to give commands and use criticism. The British group was, on measures comparing the two sets of categories, more likely to make use of accepting or praising rather than commanding or criticizing than the experienced American teachers (TRR scores). There was a greater likelihood that the present group would use lecture rather than question in the content oriented parts of the lesson, but a wider range of practice in this area as measured by the Content Cross Ratio was noted from the student groups than amongst the American groups.

There was a substantially greater probability that children's talk would be initiated by the children themselves amongst the British student groups, who were also much more likely to respond to children's ideas and feelings with immediate praise or acceptance. The student group however was much less likely to respond to children with immediate supplementary questioning than the American group, and verbal activity was much more likely to stay in the same category with the student group.

The most striking differences seem to be in the much greater occurrence of pupil initiated talk in the British students' lessons, and also the students' greater use of lecture compared with questions.

(ii) *Analysis by sex of teacher*

Table 2 gives the category totals for men teachers and women teachers.

A first analysis shows that men teachers make slightly greater use of praise and criticism and a substantially greater use of lecture, whereas women are more likely to ask questions and to accept ideas. It is however in the area of pupil talk that the most striking differences occur. In category eight (pupil talk in response to the teacher) women teachers register 121 tallies as opposed to 82 by the men teachers, but in category nine (spontaneous pupil talk) 69 tallies compared with 79 by the men.

Table 1: *Matrix for all teachers (337,617 tallies from 578 lessons)*

	1	2	3	4	5	6	7	8	9	10	Total	
1	0	0	0	0	0	0	0	0	0	0	1	Accepts feeling
2	0	1	3	3	3	1	0	1	2	2	17	Praise
3	0	1	4	8	9	1	0	1	2	3	30	Accepts ideas
4	0	0	0	13	4	1	1	43	2	14	79	Question
5	0	1	0	21	222	7	1	4	17	29	303	Lecture
6	0	0	0	2	4	13	1	5	2	11	39	Command
7	0	0	0	1	2	1	2	1	1	4	12	Criticism
8	0	8	17	12	12	4	2	36	3	6	99	Solicited children's talk
9	0	4	4	4	21	2	2	0	32	5	74	Unsolicited children's talk
10	0	1	0	16	26	9	3	8	12	270	346	Silence or non-codable

Talk = 65%	TRR = 48	TQR 8/9 = 32
Teacher Talk = 73%	TQR = 21	CCR = 50
I/D = 0·36	PIR = 43	SSR = 59
i/d = 0·94	TRR 8/9 = 80	PSSR = 39

An interesting distribution is also to be seen in the cells of the matrices (not shown here) representing prolonged talk by the children, 8–8 and 9–9. Although the women teachers produce more sustained category eight talk, the men have more sustained spontaneous pupil talk in the 9–9 cell.

To test the significance of some of these differences t tests were applied to the individual scores of men and women students. Solicited pupil response (t=2·896), I/D ratio (t=2·919), Teacher Question Ratio (t=3·232), Pupil Initiation Ratio (t=2·762) and Steady State Ratio (t=2·673) were all significant at the one per cent level of confidence.

(iii) *Analysis by age group of class*

Analysis of lessons according to age group of class was also undertaken. Extraction of some of the category totals and ratios highlights certain interesting progressions.

	Lecture (5)	Criticism (7)	Silence (10)	CCR	Pupil talk
1st year	232	16	385	43	32%
2nd year	231	18	376	45	30%
3rd year	307	16	342	50	25%
4th year	306	9	351	52	26%
5th year	341	5	338	58	23%
6th year	436	1	249	63	23%

Some of these trends appear remarkably clear. In use of lecture there is a noticeable and regular increase as the children get older, almost dividing the year groups exactly into Lower School, Middle School and Upper School. This is reflected in the gradually increasing Content Cross Ratio (CCR) which, according to Flanders, effectively measures the content-oriented parts of the lesson. The reverse of this trend is seen in the sixth year, the decline of category ten, as more and more time is devoted to open class talk and less to project and workshop activities, and the marked and regular decrease of pupil talk from 32 per cent in the first year to 23 per cent in the sixth year.

The pattern of continuous working, continuous pupil talk both of a solicited and spontaneous kind, and continuous lecture, 10–10–5–5–4–8–8–2–9–9, is markedly present in the first two years. In the third and fourth years there is a sharp rise in lecture, especially continuous lecture (5–5 cell).

The fifth year, in most cases the 'O' level or CSE group, shows some differences which are worthy of closer examination. These lessons, whilst not unlike the third and fourth year lessons in certain respects, form a bridge between these and the sixth year lessons. For example, whereas at first and second year level there were twice as many tallies in the 10–10 cell as in the 5–5 cell, and at third and fourth year level there was still a marked difference, at fifth year level there is an almost exact balance (252 compared with 254 tallies). There is very little difference between the *category* total for silence and non-verbal activity when one compares third year and fifth year lessons (342 compared with 338), but closer inspection of the full matrices shows clearer differences in distribution, especially in the 10–4 and 10–5 cells, and correspondingly in the 4–10, 5–10 cells. This suggests that whereas the silence or group working occurs more in blocks of time at third year level, there is a greater incidence of short silences between questions and periods of lecture at fifth year level. Also there is a higher frequency of questioning at fifth year level than anywhere else with a concomitant higher loading in the 4–4 cell (continuous or repeated questioning) and the 4–10 cell as mentioned above. This suggests that at fifth form level the student teachers asked more and longer questions, many of which, possibly because they were hard or thought-provoking, or because the students had greater difficulty eliciting responses from fifth year classes, were followed by a short silence. There were fewer maintained answers (8-8 cells), but for the first time the sustained spontaneous talk (9–9 cell) exceeds the 8–8 cell.

Table 2: *Category totals and ratios—men and women*

Category	Men	Women	Ratios, etc.	Men	Women
1 Accepts feeling	1	1	Talk	66%	64%
2 Praise	19	14	Teacher talk	76%	71%
3 Accepts ideas	27	34	I/D ratio	0·31	0·44
4 Question	70	89	i/d ratio	0·89	0·99
5 Lecture	331	267	TRR	47	50
6 Command	38	40	TQR	18	25
7 Criticism	14	10	PIR	49	36
8 Solicited pupil talk	82	121	TRR 8/9	79	80
9 Unsolicited pupil talk	79	69	TQR 8/9	32	32
10 Silence, etc.	339	356	CCR	51	49
			SSR	63	56
			PSSR	40	39

The sixth year lessons show a further sharp rise in lecture, and the 5–5 cell contains over twice as many tallies as the lower school matrices. Although the overall percentage of talk by the pupils is lowest of all year groups it is interesting to note that the 50 tallies in the 9–9 cell, representing continuous spontaneous pupil talk, far exceed any other year group matrix, and the Pupil Steady State Ratios (PSSR) is also higher than any other. Acceptance of ideas (category three) on the other hand is highest for any year group, and of special interest are the higher loadings in the 8–3 and 3–5 cells. This suggests a pattern of continuous information giving (5–5) spontaneous interruption (5–9–5), often prolonged as well as question and answer, and the acceptance of ideas rather than praise (8–3 rather than 8–2). Similarly there is a greater incidence of acceptance of feeling (Category one) than in any other year group.

(iv) *Analysis by subject*

Nine subjects: Maths, Physics, Chemistry, Biology, English, French, German, History and Geography, provided more than 15,000 tallies and are included under five headings (a) Mathematics (b) Sciences (c) English (d) Modern Languages (e) History and Geography.

1. Mathematics

Table 3 shows the distribution of the 50,537 tallies collected from 87 lessons reduced to millage matrix form.

Table 3: *Matrix for mathematics (50,537 tallies from 87 lessons)*

	1	2	3	4	5	6	7	8	9	10	Total	
1	0	0	0	0	0	0	0	0	0	0	0	Accepts feeling
2	0	1	1	3	4	0	0	1	1	2	13	Praise
3	0	1	3	4	6	0	0	0	1	2	18	Accepts ideas
4	0	0	0	8	3	1	1	35	3	12	63	Question
5	0	2	0	19	254	4	1	1	22	31	334	Lecture
6	0	0	0	1	3	5	1	1	1	6	19	Command
7	0	0	0	1	2	1	2	0	1	2	9	Criticism
8	0	5	10	8	10	1	1	11	3	5	54	Solicited children's talk
9	0	3	3	4	27	1	1	0	29	8	74	Unsolicited children's talk
10	0	1	0	15	26	6	2	4	14	349	417	Silence or non-codable

Talk	= 58%	TRR	= 53	TQR 8/9	= 24
Teacher Talk	= 78%	TQR	= 16	CCR	= 51
I/D	= 0·26	PIR	= 58	SSR	= 66
i/d	= 1·14	TRR 8/9	= 86	PSSR	= 31

Table 4: *Matrix for Physics (21,542 tallies from 37 lessons)*

	1	2	3	4	5	6	7	8	9	10	Total	
1	0	0	0	0	0	0	0	0	0	0	0	Accepts feeling
2	0	0	2	2	1	0	0	0	1	2	9	Praise
3	0	0	5	6	7	1	0	1	1	2	23	Accepts ideas
4	0	0	0	11	2	1	0	34	1	11	59	Question
5	0	1	0	17	213	4	1	1	20	41	298	Lecture
6	0	0	0	1	3	12	1	1	1	9	28	Command
7	0	0	0	1	2	1	2	0	0	3	8	Criticism
8	0	5	14	7	8	1	1	10	2	5	51	Solicited children's talk
9	0	2	2	2	25	1	1	0	13	4	49	Unsolicited children's talk
10	0	1	0	14	36	8	2	4	10	399	476	Silence or non-codable

Talk	= 52%	TRR	= 47	TQR 8/9	= 21
Teacher Talk	= 81%	TQR	= 17	CCR	= 47
I/D	= 0·27	PIR	= 49	SSR	= 67
i/d	= 0·88	TRR 8/9	= 84	PSSR	= 23

Mathematics students faced a dilemma in many of the schools. They had been prepared to teach using recently developed materials and techniques, yet they often found themselves in schools with traditional textbooks and syllabus. Consequently there was quite a wide range of practice. Most attempted to establish a workshop situation, which explains the high loading in category 10 (417 tallies) and in the 10–10 cell (349 tallies). Hence also the relatively high Pupil Initiation Ratio (PIR) despite the low total pupil talk sum, as most of the pupil talk was spontaneous rather than elicited by the teacher.

The high lecture total (334 tallies) can be explained by a number of different factors. A small number of mathematics teachers delivered lectures. One of these recorded almost the highest amount of lecture of the whole sample of students (over 75 per cent). Another reason for the high loading in category five is explained by the different behaviour of teachers during the workshop situation. There were those who, having set the class a problem or distributed equipment, appeared to withdraw and only responded when approached. Others saw their role as counsellor in this situation and walked round discussing problems with individuals, hence the 5–9, 9–5, 5–4, 4–8 loadings.

2. Science (Physics, Chemistry and Biology)

The breakdown of 132 Science lessons into separate matrices for Physics, Chemistry and Biology is shown in Tables 4, 5 and 6.

Again, these are often laboratory situations. There seemed to be two common types of lesson in the sciences, the double period 'experiments' lesson and the single period 'theory' lesson. To avoid the kind of unbalanced picture which might have emerged if observers had watched only, say, the first lesson of a double period, they were instructed to observe, where possible, the whole of double periods and at least one or two single periods as well. This was not always possible as some students only had double periods, the regular teacher saving the single lesson to enable him to retain contact with the class. The Flanders system is most difficult to apply in laboratory lessons and observers coded what they could hear from a favourable vantage point.

The early part of a double lesson was often explanation by the teacher (5–5–5–5) or questions revising what had been done previously related to what was going to be done during that session (4–8–8–4–8–3–5–5–5). The next 30 minutes or so, usually bridging the bell and lasting well into the second period, was the actual experiment, with the teacher, like the mathematics teachers, either walking round asking questions, offering advice, criticising dangerous behaviour (4–8–5–5–9–9–5–7–7) or staying at his bench only responding to those who came out (10–10–10–10–9–5–10–10–10), or, in extreme cases, especially with older, more unruly classes, withdrawing entirely to the adjacent preparation room and leaving the class to their experiment.

As this phase ended there would be a short chain of commands (6–6–6–6) as the children were told to put away equipment, switch off bunsens, write up what they had done, followed by 10 minutes of, often, total silence as they wrote their account (10–10–10–10). Finally the class would gather round the bench of the teacher either for a demonstration of what should have happened (5–5–10–10–10–5–5–10–10), or, more likely, a part demonstration, part question and answer period (5–6–10–10–4–8–3–4–8–3–4–8–3–6–6–10–10) to

Table 5: *Matrix for Chemistry (40,249 tallies from 68 lessons)*

	1	2	3	4	5	6	7	8	9	10	Total	
1	0	0	0	0	0	0	0	0	0	0	0	Accepts feeling
2	0	0	4	2	3	1	0	0	2	4	17	Praise
3	0	0	3	6	8	1	0	1	1	3	23	Accepts ideas
4	0	0	0	11	2	1	0	39	1	12	66	Question
5	0	1	0	17	188	7	2	1	12	35	263	Lecture
6	0	0	0	2	5	23	1	1	4	17	53	Command
7	0	0	0	1	3	2	4	1	2	7	19	Criticism
8	0	7	12	9	8	2	2	9	2	5	56	Solicited children's talk
9	0	7	2	2	16	3	3	0	11	4	48	Unsolicited children's talk
10	0	1	0	15	31	14	6	5	13	368	454	Silence or non-codable

Talk	= 55%	TRR	= 36	TQR 8/9 = 32
Teacher Talk	= 81%	TQR	= 20	CCR = 44
I/D	= 0.32	PIR	= 46	SSR = 62
i/d	= 0.55	TRR 8/9	= 74	PSSR = 19

Table 6: *Matrix for Biology (16,079 tallies from 27 lessons)*

	1	2	3	4	5	6	7	8	9	10	Total	
1	0	0	0	0	0	0	0	0	0	0	0	Accepts feeling
2	0	0	5	3	3	1	0	0	2	3	18	Praise
3	0	1	3	5	8	0	0	1	1	1	20	Accepts ideas
4	0	0	0	9	2	1	1	44	1	8	65	Question
5	0	1	0	16	179	8	1	1	15	31	252	Lecture
6	0	0	0	3	3	43	1	1	6	24	81	Command
7	0	0	0	2	2	2	2	1	2	4	14	Criticism
8	0	10	10	8	7	4	3	15	3	6	66	Solicited children's talk
9	0	6	1	5	20	6	3	0	19	6	66	Unsolicited children's talk
10	0	1	0	14	26	17	3	4	17	336	419	Silence or non-codable

Talk	= 58%	TRR	= 29	TQR 8/9	= 32
Teacher Talk	= 77%	TQR	= 21	CCR	= 43
I/D	= 0·30	PIR	= 50	SSR	= 61
i/d	= 0·40	TRR 8/9	= 63	PSSR	= 26

finish off. This pattern is detected in particular for most of the double Chemistry lessons, often for Biology but with a greater directiveness, and less frequently for Physics, where the higher incidence of note dictation has produced higher tallies in the 5–5 and 10–10 cells reflecting a pattern 5–5–5–10–10–10–10–5–5–5–10–10–10–10.

3. English

Table 7 shows the 53,673 tallies collected from 92 English lessons in matrix form.

Common activities described in the lesson reports on English lessons are reading aloud, debate or class discussion, drama and creative writing. The emphasis laid on the development of oral skills by most of the sample can be seen from the very high loadings of categories eight and nine (158 and 112 respectively), the lower rate of teacher talk, and the large number of tallies in the continuous pupil talk cells, 8–8 and 9–9, which at 105 and 67 massively exceed those found in any other matrix.

Activities like reading poetry or prose aloud and debating serve to swell the continuous pupil talk cells considerably. Debates produce long chains of 9 interspersed with the teacher's contributions—9–9–9–9–9–5–5–9–9–9–9. Despite the high loadings in pupil talk cells this has not been achieved by high use of questioning, which was the case in modern language lessons as described below. The 4–8 cell is not excessively populated nor is the 6–8 cell (command followed by answer) heavily tallied. The main device for achieving this sustained pupil talk lay in the techniques described above, where a single command or statement was sufficient to establish a lengthy pupil contribution or series of contributions.

Flow chart analysis of the English matrix shows a 10–5–9–9–6–4–8–8–3 movement. Some individual students achieved quite different patterns, and on surface analysis there seemed to be a greater variety of pattern in English lessons than was the case in other subjects which appeared to make use of a smaller number of stereotyped lesson formats. A number of English students talked approximately half the time as compared with the mean of 73 per cent for the whole group. In one case there was as little as 44 per cent of the talk by the teacher and 56 per cent by the class.

One other area where English teachers are distinguished is the infrequently occurring category one (acceptance of feeling). With 3·37 tallies per thousand the English group shows a much higher incidence of this kind of teacher talk than any other group in the present sample. Most frequently this would occur in poetry lessons and would often tend to be clarification of the feelings, as when children gave their description of the sadness or happiness evoked in them by a poem and the teacher enlarged on this.

4. Modern languages (French and German)

Modern language lessons can be coded using the existing Flanders system, but then the important information about the language in which the interaction takes place is lost. To avoid this loss of important information the present writer has designed and used a simple variation of the Flanders system (Wragg 1970c and 1970d). The ten categories are

Table 7: *Matrix for English (53,673 tallies from 92 lessons)*

	1	2	3	4	5	6	7	8	9	10	Total	
1	1	0	0	1	0	0	0	0	0	0	3	Accepts feeling
2	0	1	3	3	2	1	0	1	3	2	15	Praise
3	0	1	4	7	6	1	0	2	3	2	24	Accepts ideas
4	0	0	0	10	4	1	0	37	3	8	64	Question
5	0	1	0	14	201	5	2	4	14	17	259	Lecture
6	0	0	0	2	3	14	1	3	3	10	36	Command
7	0	0	0	1	2	1	3	1	2	5	13	Criticism
8	0	6	12	11	9	3	1	105	5	5	158	Solicited children's talk
9	1	5	5	5	18	3	1	0	67	7	112	Unsolicited children's talk
10	0	1	0	11	13	8	5	5	13	259	315	Silence or non-codable

Talk	= 68%	TRR	= 46	TQR 8/9	= 37
Teacher Talk	= 61%	TQR	= 20	CCR	= 42
I/D	= 0·34	PIR	= 42	SSR	= 67
i/d	= 0·86	TRR 8/9	= 79	PSSR	= 64

extended to twenty, the first 10 being the Flanders categories, and categories 11 to 20 being the same categories if used in the foreign language. The full description is given below:

Adapting Flanders category system to a foreign language classroom

Speaker	Category Number Language		Category Description
	Native	Foreign	
T e a c h e r	1	11	Accepts feelings: accepts and clarifies the feeling tone of the students in a non-threatening manner. Feelings may be positive or negative. Predicting and recalling feelings are included.
	2	12	Praises or encourages: praises or encourages student action or behaviour. Jokes that release tension, not at the expense of another individual, nodding head or saying 'uh huh?' or 'go on' or their equivalent in the foreign language are included.
	3	13	Accepts or uses ideas of students: clarifying, building, or developing ideas or suggestions by a student. As teacher brings more of his own ideas into play, shift to category five or fifteen.
	4	14	Asks questions: asking a question about content or procedure with the intent that a student answer.
	5	15	Lectures: giving facts or opinions about content or procedure with the intent that a student answer.
	6	16	Gives directions: directions, commands, or orders with which a student is expected to comply.
	7	17	Criticises or justifies authority: statements, intended to change student behaviour, from non-acceptable to acceptable pattern; bawling someone out; stating why the teacher is doing what he is doing, extreme self-reference.
P u p i l	8	18	Student talk-response: talk by students in response to teacher. Teacher initiates the contact or solicits student statement.
	9	19	Student talk-initiation: talk by students, which they initiate. If 'calling on' student is only to indicate who may talk next, observer must decide whether student wanted to talk. If he did, use this category.
	10	20	Silence or confusion, pauses, short periods of silence, and periods of confusion in which communication cannot be understood by the observer. Use category 20 following talk in the foreign language.

Lessons are tallied in the same way, but the resulting data have to be tabulated on a 20 x 20 matrix, which is effectively four 10 x 10 matrices side by side.

Figure 1 shows what would be the case for a French lesson.

Figure 1: *Arrangement of a 20 x 20 Foreign Language matrix*

	1 to 10	11 to 20
1 to 10	English followed by English	English followed by French
11 to 20	French followed by English	French followed by French

Most of the normal calculations can be made and a computer program was specially written to compile a 20 x 20 matrix. It is essential that an observer using the system be fluent in the languages being observed, and this was the case in the present research.

Analysis of Table 8 shows that of all talk 52 per cent was in English and 48 per cent in the foreign language, an even balance. There are on closer inspection, however, interesting differences when the interactions in the native and foreign languages are compared.

Table 8: *20 x 20 matrix of foreign language lessons (47,862 tallies from 81 lessons)*

	1	2	3	4	5	6	7	8	9	10	11	12
1	0	0	0	0	0	0	0	0	0	0	0	0
2	0	0	0	1	1	1	0	0	0	2	0	0
3	0	1	1	5	6	2	0	1	2	5	0	0
4	0	0	0	7	3	2	0	24	1	16	0	0
5	0	0	0	12	56	8	1	2	7	19	0	0
6	0	0	0	2	4	10	1	2	2	17	0	0
7	0	0	0	1	0	1	2	0	1	5	0	0
8	0	2	14	6	6	2	1	6	2	4	0	0
9	0	1	5	3	11	2	2	0	9	4	0	0
10	0	0	0	12	15	11	3	6	10	103	0	0
11	0	0	0	0	0	0	0	0	0	0	0	0
12	0	0	0	0	0	1	0	0	0	0	0	0
13	0	0	0	2	1	1	0	0	0	0	0	1
14	0	0	0	2	1	1	0	5	1	0	0	0
15	0	0	0	6	13	3	0	2	3	0	0	0
16	0	0	0	0	0	0	0	0	0	0	0	0
17	0	0	0	0	0	0	0	0	0	0	0	0
18	0	3	4	6	5	4	1	0	1	0	0	7
19	0	0	1	0	1	0	0	0	1	0	0	0
20	0	0	0	4	3	3	1	1	3	0	0	0

First of all, pupil talk is much higher in the foreign language blocks (39 per cent compared with 24 per cent) suggesting that the teachers use the foreign language parts of the lesson largely for oral practice, a supposition supported both by the lesson reports and the loadings in the 14–18, 18–18 and 18–14 cells. Secondly, teachers are very much more 'indirect' whether on the I/D or i/d ratio in the foreign language than in the native language parts of the lesson. For the foreign language parts the I/D is 0·81 compared with 0·56 and the i/d is 1·89 compared with 0·57. This can be explained by a number of reasons. Very little use is

	13	14	15	16	17	18	19	20	Total	*In English*
1	0	0	0	0	0	0	0	0	1	Accepts feeling
2	0	0	1	0	0	1	0	0	8	Praise
3	0	1	3	0	0	1	0	0	27	Accepts ideas
4	0	1	2	0	0	13	0	0	68	Question
5	0	2	14	1	0	3	1	0	125	Lecture
6	0	1	3	1	0	9	0	0	51	Command
7	0	0	0	0	0	0	0	0	12	Criticism
8	0	2	2	0	0	1	0	0	48	Solicited children's talk
9	0	1	3	0	0	0	1	0	43	Unsolicited children's talk
10	0	3	6	1	0	6	1	0	177	Silence or non-codable
										In foreign language
11	0	0	0	0	0	0	0	0	0	Accepts feeling
12	2	2	1	1	0	1	0	1	10	Praise
13	0	7	4	2	0	2	0	5	26	Accepts ideas
14	0	13	1	0	0	19	0	17	60	Question
15	0	8	42	2	0	6	1	13	100	Lecture
16	0	1	1	1	0	12	0	3	19	Command
17	0	0	0	0	0	0	0	0	0	Criticism
18	21	7	9	7	0	40	1	8	123	Solicited children's talk
19	1	0	2	0	0	0	5	2	13	Unsolicited children's talk
20	0	10	8	3	0	10	2	39	88	Silence or non-codable

made of either acceptance of feeling or criticism in the foreign language. It was only on extremely rare occasions that teachers stayed in the foreign language to criticise unsatisfactory answers or undesirable behaviour. Usually they automatically switched back to their native language. In addition there is a less frequent use of command in the foreign language (19 compared with 51).

A very noticeable feature of the pupil talk which was observed at the pilot stage (Wragg 1970c) is the considerable imbalance between solicited and unsolicited pupil talk in the foreign language compared with the native language, as can be seen below with the pilot study figures for comparison. The pilot study data are not strictly comparable as they were all collected towards the end of teaching practice whereas the 1969/70 data were collected throughout the term, but nevertheless the position is clear. When pupils are talking in English there is a balance between solicited and unsolicited talk, but in the foreign language parts of the lesson there is considerable dependence on the teacher, causing a huge imbalance.

		1968/69	1969/70
(Native Language)	Solicited children's talk (8)	30	48
	Unsolicited children's talk (9)	30	43
(Foreign language)	Solicited children's talk (18)	171	123
	Unsolicited children's talk (19)	3	13

Table 8 shows a flow 14–18–13–14–18–18–13 which for some teachers was a very mechanical pattern as responses were repeated and occasionally praised, all in the foreign language.

5. History and Geography

Tables 9 and 10 show the matrices for History and Geography, both high in talk with low category 10.

Geography registers more lecture than any other subject and is also low on pupil talk especially category eight. History on the other hand is high on category eight and almost as high as English on category nine. It also has a much higher Pupil Steady State Ratio than Geography, suggesting that there was much more prolonged talk by the children. Inspection of the 8–8 and 9–9 cells show that this was the case (44 and 45 for History compared with 13 and 17 for Geography).

Much of the lessons in both subjects consisted of continuous lecture, hence the heavily tallied 5–5 cell, but there was extensive use, especially in History, of question and answer. The difference between History and Geography is that the History teachers obtained more and longer responses (8–8 cell), but the Geography teachers made greater use of praise and acceptance of ideas, producing a 4–8–3–4–8–3 cycle as opposed to the 4–8–9–3–6–8–9–9–5 pattern of the History teachers.

A small number of History and Geography teachers appeared to have perfected a programmed instruction style of teaching which was mechanically regular, producing a cycle of (a) small unit of information followed by (b) short question followed by (c) short answer, praise, acceptance of ideas and (d) the next 'frame'—5–5–4–8–2–3–5–5–4–8–2–3–5–5–4–8–2–3—a regular and predictable pattern.

Although many of the Geographers produced long spells of uninterrupted lecture, as did a smaller number of Historians, a few interesting variations occurred. Some students 'seeded' both their questions and their acceptance of ideas with supplementary information such as 'Why did the general decide to march that night, and remember how far they were from the capital', or 'Yes, that's right, the army was hungry, and what's more, as someone pointed out earlier, there was not likely to be food in that area.' This kind of exchange produced a pattern of 4–4–5–5–8–8–8–3–3–5–5–3 rather than 5–5–5–5–5–5–5–5 or 5–5–5–5–5–4–8–5–5–5–5.

Fairly extensive use of supplementary visual material is reported by the observers. The presence of pictures, slides or models does not necessarily change interaction patterns however. Some teachers still lectured about their pictures or models and others asked questions about them. With those who adopted the programmed instruction format described above, the pictures were often part of the 'frame' and the lesson almost became an illustrated programme.

In many ways the Flanders system, whilst less than ideal for Maths and Science, is very well suited to the Geography, History, English, Modern Language lessons, where at the present time a great deal of work is done in the whole class situation.

(v) *Analysis by sex grouping of class*

For this analysis schools were divided into boys' schools, girls' schools and mixed schools.

Table 9. *Matrix for History (47,592 tallies from 82 lessons)*

	1	2	3	4	5	6	7	8	9	10	Total	
1	0	0	0	0	0	0	0	0	0	0	0	Accepts feeling
2	0	1	5	4	3	0	0	1	3	1	18	Praise
3	0	1	6	11	12	1	0	2	3	2	39	Accepts ideas
4	0	0	0	18	5	1	1	53	3	13	93	Question
5	0	1	0	26	290	4	2	4	23	24	375	Lecture
6	0	0	0	2	3	10	1	2	3	7	27	Command
7	0	0	0	1	3	1	3	1	2	3	14	Criticism
8	0	9	22	14	12	2	2	44	4	4	113	Solicited children's talk
9	0	6	5	5	26	2	2	0	45	3	96	Unsolicited children's talk
10	0	0	0	12	20	5	3	6	10	166	224	Silence or non-codable

Talk	= 78%	TRR	= 58	TQR 8/9	= 34
Teacher Talk	= 73%	TQR	= 20	CCR	= 60
I/D	= 0·36	PIR	= 46	SSR	= 58
i/d	= 1·39	TRR 8/9	= 82	PSSR	= 43

Inspection of the category totals in Table 11 reveals considerable differences in the time spent on lecturing. There was less lecture in the girls' schools (257 tallies) than in the mixed schools (322), much more questioning (100) compared with 75 (boys) and 72 (mixed), and much more solicited pupil response (122 compared with 100 and 91). On the other hand there was less spontaneous pupil response in girls' schools (56 compared with 69 and 85) and very much less use of criticism by the teacher (four compared with 17 [boys] and 13 [mixed]).

Tentatively one might propose that the student teachers in the sample were affected by the sex of children in the school and this led to greater use of lecture in boys' schools as well as less balance between solicited and unsolicited talk. Similarly girls' schools seemed to produce greater use of questioning, less use of criticism and lower occurrence of spontaneous talk by the children. This is only a tentative suggestion of the basis on the comparisons made above, and it is one which merits further and more thorough investigation.

Whether this reflects an 'easier' or more congenial atmosphere it is not possible to say, but mixed schools show a higher incidence of spontaneous children's talk. The full matrices (not shown here) reveal a markedly heavier tallying in the sustained spontaneous talk cell (9–9) of the mixed schools (40 tallies) especially compared with the girls' schools (19 tallies). This might explain the complaints made annually by some women students about the difficulty of generating class discussion in girls' schools. On the other hand there is a very much higher immediate acceptance of ideas loading (8–3 cell) for girls' schools (30 tallies compared with 16 in boys' schools and 14 in mixed schools), but this may be

Table 10. *Matrix for Geography (30,544 tallies from 53 lessons)*

	1	2	3	4	5	6	7	8	9	10	Total	
1	0	0	0	0	0	0	0	0	0	0	0	Accepts feeling
2	0	2	6	5	6	0	0	1	3	2	25	Praise
3	0	2	8	8	14	0	0	1	2	4	39	Accepts ideas
4	0	1	0	12	4	1	1	43	6	14	80	Question
5	0	1	1	27	338	7	2	2	18	29	425	Lecture
6	0	0	0	2	5	10	1	1	2	8	28	Command
7	0	0	0	1	2	1	3	1	1	3	13	Criticism
8	0	11	17	9	10	1	1	13	3	3	67	Solicited children's talk
9	0	8	7	4	20	2	2	0	27	2	72	Unsolicited children's talk
10	0	1	0	12	26	6	3	6	10	185	250	Silence or non-codable

Talk = 75%	TRR = 61	TQR 8/9 = 30
Teacher Talk = 81%	TQR = 16	CCR = 63
I/D = 0·31	PIR = 52	SSR = 60
i/d = 1·56	TRR 8/9 = 88	PSSR = 28

Table 11: *Category totals—sex grouping of class*

Category	Boys' schools	Girls' schools	Mixed schools
1 Accepts feeling . . .	0	2	1
2 Praise	19	15	16
3 Accepts ideas . . .	31	45	24
4 Question	75	100	72
5 Lecture	297	257	322
6 Command	43	37	37
7 Criticism	17	4	13
8 Solicited children's talk . .	100	122	91
9 Unsolicited children's talk .	69	56	85
10 Silence, etc.	349	363	338

either the cause or effect of the much more heavily tallied category eight (solicited pupil response).

To some extent differences between boys' and girls' schools reflect the differences between men and women teachers discussed above.

(vi) *Analysis by stage of teaching practice*

The teaching practice period was divided into four periods, labelled period A, period B, period C and period D. Each of these consisted of twelve school days.

The category totals in table 12 show in more detail how period D is in many respects different from the other three periods. Most conspicuous is the rise in category 10 after the gradual increases over the first three periods. This would be difficult to explain without the lesson notes which suggest a higher incidence of 'project' type lessons in the late stages of the term. It does appear, therefore, that students are more likely to work informally in small groups towards the end of their teaching practice, but will possibly use the earlier periods to establish rapport and gain confidence.

Period C registers the highest amount of lecture and the highest amount of continuous lecture (5–5 cell). It could be that it is at this stage, just after half term, that the student has

Table 12: *Category totals—stage of teaching practice*

Category	Period A	Period B	Period C	Period D
1 Accepts feeling	1	1	1	0
2 Praise	21	18	15	11
3 Accepts ideas	27	34	32	24
4 Question	93	86	71	64
5 Lecture	302	292	328	258
6 Command	41	46	36	33
7 Criticism	11	13	12	12
8 Solicited children's talk	115	118	82	89
9 Unsolicited children's talk . . .	77	63	83	75
10 Silence, etc.	316	329	340	434
(5–5) Cell - continuous lecture . . .	226	211	246	178
(8–8) Cell - sustained solicited pupil talk . .	46	45	26	35
(9–9) Cell - sustained unsolicited pupil talk . .	35	24	36	28

become more confident and therefore talks longer and more fluently. Consequently there is an important change in the pupil steady state cells of the full matrices (8–8 and 9–9). Although the 8–8 cell shows the lowest total at any stage of the term, the 9–9 cell is at its highest.

In many ways this analysis by stage of teaching practice is amongst the most interesting ways of looking at student teachers, as it can describe some features of their development over the term. It would be a worthwhile project to investigate this developmental aspect on its own to see if the above findings and suppositions are supported.

Since the overwhelming majority of students on the sample did their teaching practice in Grammar Schools, separate analyses for other types of school and comparisons between schools have not been made.

(b) Analysis of individual students' scores

In addition to analysing the data by groups, certain comparisons have been made between the scores obtained by students for various of the presage, process and product variables.

(i) *Comparison of presage and process variables*

For a sample of this size a product moment of $r = \cdot194$ is significant at the five per cent level (*) and $r = \cdot253$ is significant at the one per cent level (**). Table 13 shows correlations between presage and process variables found to be significant at the one per cent level of confidence. Since 1431 separate intercorrelations have been calculated, a number of significant relationships are to be expected by chance.

The correlations between Cattell A (warmth) and certain kinds of accepting behaviour (ID ratio and Teacher Question Ratio), and both Cattell I (sensitivity) and the Aesthetic value and high sustained pupil talk (Pupil Steady State Ratio, category eight and negative correlation with teacher talk) are especially interesting as they do appear to have a logical basis. Such links between measured personality traits and observed classroom behaviour are worthy of further study. Davies (1961) found a positive link between Cattell A and Flanders categories one and three.

Table 13: *Summary of correlations between presage variables and process variables found to be significant at the one per cent level*

		Cat 3	Cat 4	Cat 6	Cat 8	Cat 10	% Teacher Talk	I/D	TQR	SSR	PSSR
1	Cattell A							·272	·313		
8	Cattell I				·271		−·370				·317
12	Cattell O			·267							
15	Cattell Q3						·277				
16	Cattell Q4						−·256				
18	Economic value						·270				−·337
19	Aesthetic value				·304		−·422				·268
20	Social value		·264						·282		
23	Fluency	·271									
28	Degree class					−·392				−·272	

The Torrance test scores show a small number of interesting relationships. There are correlations between fluency scores and acceptance of ideas (r=·271**), use of question (r=214*), and use of commands (r=·223*). Flexibility correlates with use of commands and solicited pupil talk (r=·225* and r=·228*). Originality correlates negatively with Teacher Talk (r=— ·196*), suggesting the original teacher is more willing to listen to children talking.

Finally, the negative correlation between class of degree and category 10 (r=— ·392**) either suggests that the more academic teachers talk more, which may be the case, or it may be an artifact due to the Arts/Science differences both in level of qualifications and classroom patterns. (Further analysis of relationships between some of the presage and process variables is reported in 'The creative thinking abilities of students in teacher training programmes' by D. Evans, final report of a project sponsored by the Social Science Research Council, October 1970).

A canonical correlation analysis provided no clear factors, thus confirming that the presage and process variables in the research largely measured separate domains.

(ii) *The relation of product variables to both presage and process variables*

Variable 54 (composite of ratings of effectiveness by schools and tutors) was used to group the 102 students in the sample into three groups rated above average, average and below average. One way analysis of variance was used to test the significance of the differences in the scores obtained on the presage and process variables by the three groups. For the F ratio to be significant with groups of this size it must exceed 3·09 at the five per cent level and 4·81 at the one per cent level. Significant F ratios were obtained for presage variables 9 (Cattell L) 15 (Cattell Q3) 24 (Torrance Flexibility) and 28 (class of degree). For Cattell Q3 (self-control) the F ratio was 8·41**, and both the above average and below average groups had a higher mean score than the average group, i.e. tended to show greater self-control. This might suggest that for student teachers to be self-controlled can be both good and bad. Start (1966) reported good teachers to be low on Q3, whereas Erickson (1954) found them high on the same variable.

On Cattell L the above average teachers were highest (more trusting) and the below average lowest (more paranoid), giving an F ratio of 3·57*. This supports the finding of Start (1966) with experienced teachers.

On variable 24, Torrance flexibility score, the above average group scored higher than both the average and below average groups who had nearly identical mean scores, and the F ratio was 3·21*. Finally class of degree, usually known to the raters, was also significant with an F ratio of 5·23** with the above average group tending to have the best degrees and the below average group the poorest.

Although no significant F ratios were obtained between classroom behaviour measures and ratings of effectiveness, there were a number of significant correlation coefficients. Use of criticism (category seven) correlates negatively with Tutors' ratings (r=·267**) and composite rating (r=— ·223*) though not with schools' ratings (r=— ·140 n.s.). This suggests that tutors are less likely to favour those students who make greater use of criticism. For many student teachers, extensive use of criticism, especially in the later stages of teaching practice, often occurs in classes where the teacher has lost control and has to shout and threaten in order to restore some kind of order.

The second classroom variable to correlate with measures of effectiveness was solicited pupil talk (category eight). This correlated r=·251* with schools' ratings, r=·201* with tutors' ratings and r=·250* with composite ratings, suggesting that both supervising parties value high solicited talk. It is interesting to compare this with the very low correlation between ratings and category nine which are $r = \cdot 000$ n.s., $r = \cdot 010$ n.s., and $r = \cdot 005$ n.s. for schools, tutors and total respectively.

On the whole there is the expected low incidence of significant relationships between measures of effectiveness and presage and process variables.

(iii) *The factor analysis*

In the interests of parsimony it was decided that a factor analysis would reduce a large amount of data to something more manageable conceptually.

Before a factor analysis could be undertaken certain variables were excluded. It is important in factor analysis to avoid including variables which are not independent of other variables, otherwise spurious factors can easily be generated involving only the mutually dependent variables. Since the scores on the Allport-Vernon-Lindzey Study of Values are ipsative, it was decided to omit the Religious value score which was found to correlate negatively with almost all the other values. The total score was omitted from the Torrance tests as this was obviously dependent on the part scores. All the ratios based on the separate students' millage matrices were omitted as these had a degree of dependence on the category totals (variables 39 to 50 inclusive), but the flexibility factor which was based on four separate matrices was retained. Finally variable 54, the composite rating of effectiveness, was also left out because of its dependence on the school and tutor ratings. This left 39 variables out of the original 54.

The analysis was performed on the Atlas computer as described using the Hallworth program with rotation to simple structure according to the varimax criterion. Fourteen factors were produced, none of these large, accounting between them for 73 per cent of the variance. The five largest factors, each accounting for six per cent or more of the variance, and between them covering over a third of the total variance (34 per cent) are given below in Table 14.

Factor I is almost entirely a classroom behaviour factor. The high loadings on categories three, four and eight suggest a teaching style with emphasis on question answer and acceptance of children's ideas. There is an association with class of degree but a high loading in the reverse direction on silence. This factor is perhaps easier to name if the signs are reversed. It might be called a *teacher-controlled classroom interaction factor*, teacher-controlled because of the lack of significant loading on category nine. The degree class and acceptance of ideas loadings would suggest that these high talk lessons were relevant to the academic content of the subject. The absence of a loading on category seven would also suggest this.

Factor IX is also largely a classroom behaviour factor but with the emphasis on unsolicited pupil response, and praise and acceptance of feeling. The loadings on the Aesthetic value and Flexibility Factor make it look close to the pattern frequently observed in English lessons. The high loading on *unsolicited* pupil talk and acceptance of the feelings expressed, added to the teacher's ability to be flexible, justify this being named a *pupil-oriented classroom interaction factor*.

Factors II and IV are largely personality factors and *Factor III* is clearly a creativity Factor since there are no loadings of any consequence other than the Torrance scores.

(iv) *The cluster analysis*

Q-mode analysis, whereby analysis is conducted *across* the subject profiles rather than *down* the scores on the variables, enables typologies or taxonomies to be constructed.

A computer program developed by Mather (1969) was used on classroom data (variables 29-51). In this programme an R-mode analysis is performed first of all and this reduces the number of variables by combining those showing the highest correlations. Thereafter Q-mode analyses successively pair together the students whose classroom profiles are most similar until the whole group has been combined.

Cluster analysis confirmed many of the inferences made from the subject group millage matrices above. A large cluster of languages teachers, characterized by high categories two, four, six and eight and low category five, Pupil Initiation Ratio, Steady State Ratio and Flexibility Factor, was produced. Another sizeable cluster characterized by the workshop pattern of low categories two, five, eight and nine and high category 10 consisted almost entirely of teachers of Art, Maths and Sciences.

A third cluster, high in category five, eight and Pupil Steady State Ratio was largely History and Geography teachers.

English teachers tended either to stay out of the clustering process until the end, or to be attached to all the other clusters, showing how varied their patterns could be.

Separate cluster analysis of men and women students showed that the clusters of men teachers were less clearly defined by subjects than those of the women.

Table 14: *Five main factors obtained by Varimax rotation*

	Variable	I	II	III	VI	IX
1	Cattell A (warmth)		−42			
3	Cattell C (maturity)		−68			
4	Cattell E (dominance)				−68	
5	Cattell F (enthusiasm)		−60		−32	
6	Cattell G (conscientiousness)				+74	
7	Cattell H (adventurousness)		−65			
8	Cattell I (sensitiveness)				+25	
11	Cattell M (sophistication)				−71	
12	Cattell O (insecurity)		+38			
13	Cattell Q1 (radicalness)				−33	
14	Cattell Q2 (self-sufficiency)		−30			
15	Cattell Q3 (self-control)		−49			
16	Cattell Q4 (tenseness)		+79			
17	Theoretical value				−52	
19	Aesthetic value					+33
21	Political value		−35		−32	
23	Fluency			+91		
24	Flexibility			+91		
25	Originality			+88		
28	Degree Class	−39				+25
29	Acceptance of feeling (Flanders 1)					+84
30	Praise (2)					+27
31	Acceptance of Ideas (3)	−79				
32	Question (4)	−85				
34	Command (6)	−26				
36	Solicited Pupil response (8)	−73				
37	Unsolicited Pupil response (9)					+84
38	Silence (10)	+60				
51	Flexibility Factor					+29
	% Variance	7	8	7	6	6

(v) *Multivariate analysis of variance*

Multivariate analysis of variance was used to study the effects of factors such as sex of teacher, subject being taught and age group of class on dependent variables such as teacher behaviour in the classroom.

As in many educational research problems not designed specifically for analysis of variance procedures, there are accompanying problems. A full factorial design allowing for two categories of sex, six categories of year group and nine categories of subject produces a $2 \times 6 \times 9$ or 108 cell model. Addition of 'type of school' produces a $2 \times 6 \times 9 \times 4$ or 432 cell design which would clearly lead to many empty cells.

It was decided therefore to concentrate analysis on lessons given in Grammar schools, which were the vast majority, and to reduce the number of subjects to four groups instead of nine separate subjects. This produced a $2 \times 6 \times 4$ or 48 cell design and 410 of the original 578 lessons could be analysed.

A repeated measures design was not possible, but the question of teacher variance was considered by means of the Flexibility Factor.

The subject groups were reduced to four, these being (1) Maths, Physics, Chemistry, Biology; (2) English; (3) French and German; (4) History and Geography. This was done because these tend to be the usual subject groupings for individual students, e.g. 'Modern Languages', 'Sciences', and because they have a certain conceptual identity.

To overcome the problem of unequal numbers in the cells a multivariate analysis of variance programme called GUMA was used. This programme was specially written by Dr Brian Baughan of London University for designs with unequal numbers in the cells.

It was decided to use nine of the 10 Flanders category totals as dependent variables. Category one, acceptance of feeling, was not included because of its very skewed distribution.

The effects of the sex of the teacher were discussed above. Age of class being taught was shown to have a significant effect on lecture, command, criticism, unsolicited children's talk and category ten (silence etc.). This confirmed the observations made earlier when the data were analysed according to age of class.

Subject being taught exerted massive influence on frequency of occurrence of all the Flanders categories except praise and criticism. The colossal influence of the subject on the nature of classroom interaction is certainly the most striking and important finding in the multivariate analysis of variance.

V CONCLUSIONS

(a) Research design and procedures

As this was a first live study of a large number of student teachers, it was difficult to decide what should be controlled for in an area where the number of significant variables was high and complex. In practice, there was some control for stage of teaching practice and age group of class. Future studies could well concentrate on particular subject areas and type of school, as well as other priorities.

The test materials used in the present research were satisfactory but certain reservations must be expressed. The Cattell 16PF would have been better if the longer and more reliable forms A or B had been administered. The Torrance tests are not entirely satisfactory for reasons stated earlier. It is a matter of some urgency that valid and reliable creativity tests for intelligent adults are developed in this country. The AH5 produced little which proved to be related to other measures.

The Flanders system was shown to have a number of limitations. The main inadequacy of the Flanders system was shown to be in the laboratory/workshop situation. In practice, most teachers having private consultations with individual pupils could be heard by the observer, except when there was considerable noise, or when the teacher spoke very softly, and it must be assumed, because of the 'ripple effect' that these private interactions had some effect on classroom climate, since others could hear them. The low incidence of pupil talk in these lessons, however, could easily lead to the usually unjustified conclusion that children did not talk, because the Flanders system looks only at teacher-pupil interaction, and only codes pupil-pupil interactions when these occur in open class discussion.

Category one, an infrequently appearing category, is retained by Flanders because he feels that acceptance of feeling is significant where it occurs. It would be worthwhile investigating a little more closely the effects of this category. It is the writer's experience both from personal observation and from training almost 100 observers in three years, that it is a category which is frequently missed. The reliability of observers for category one is low, yet overall inter-observer reliability using the Flanders system tends to be very high, when observers have been trained thoroughly. This is because, out of 500 tallies, one observer may record ten tallies in category one, another five and, a third none at all. These differences are minimized in the Scott formula calculations as they only amount to one or two per cent.

The present research did not support Flanders' claim that category three, accepting ideas, shows few differences according to subject matter. Subjects tended to polarize with Maths and Sciences low and some Arts subjects high. This may reflect differences in English and American teaching patterns as mentioned above.

The Content Cross Ratio needs closer analysis. It was shown in the present research to be correlated significantly with class of degree, suggesting that the better qualified students recorded more interactions in this area. It still needs to be validated more rigorously, however, and this might be done by two observers coding separately 'subject-oriented talk' and Flanders categories. This ought to show how meaningful the term 'content cross' really is. Student 39 for example, an English teacher who had long class discussions and recorded higher category one and nine totals than any other student, has a Content Cross Ratio of 34 which is one of the lowest, largely because of the heavily tallied 8-8 and 9-9 cells which are outside the Content Cross area. Yet few would have disputed that these extended class discussions were relevant to the task. For a student like this the term 'content cross' has little meaning.

Perhaps greater standardization of lesson reports might have been advisable. It was thought best to leave this to the discretion of the observer who had been trained in what to look for and knew the kind of information needed. Nevertheless there were differences in lesson reports. Some were long and detailed, others short and less detailed. This caused few problems in practice, but if more information were needed about classroom organization and its relationship to Flanders data, a more formal way of reporting the lesson would be essential.

A number of category systems already in use might be more suitable for certain studies of student teachers than the Flanders system.

If secondary student teachers are to be studied by subject specialism it would probably be better to use a system specially designed for that subject. The present research used an adaptation of Flanders for observing Modern Language lessons. Moskowitz (1966) has also developed a system for describing foreign language lessons.

A number of category systems have been specially devised for science lessons. Altman (1969) used a simple system for describing science lessons which had levels of children's cognitive behaviour such as 'recall facts', 'make observations', 'see relationships', 'hypothesize', and 'test hypothesis', as well as communication methods such as demonstration, directed laboratory work and non-directed laboratory work.

Hunter (1958) devised another system which included a wider range of pupil talk categories such as one needs in science lessons—(8) responds to another pupil; (10) initiates talk to another pupil; (11) talk between pupils whilst they use materials.

Matthews (1959) devised a science curriculum assessment system with separate schedules for observation of teacher or pupils. For the teacher there are two separate categories depending on whether he interacts with a subgroup of less than seven children or with the whole group. The children have separate categories for lesson-related and non-lesson-related behaviour.

Parakh (1967) developed his system for Biology lessons. It is a more complicated system to use than the others in science, but it has interesting categories such as 'teacher examines child's activities e.g. checking slide under microscope', and 'teacher gives information about the nature of science'. In view of the complexity of the system, however, it seems to have much less to recommend it than the other science systems.

Wright (1966) designed a system for mathematics lessons which seems a difficult one to use. It identifies such activities as 'formal proof of a new concept', 'informal examination or discovery of a new concept' and 'statement of a new concept'. For a study of student teachers using newer methods of mathematics teaching it might be better than some of the general category systems.

Clements (1967) focused on Art lessons and developed categories to describe questions a teacher might ask children in Art Lessons. These included Process Recall Questions such as, 'How did you get that effect?' and Intent Questions like, 'What do you intend to do here?'. Provided the observer can hear individual interactions with children in the Art room, this might again be more appropriate than a general system.

At least two investigators have looked at ways of describing classrooms where individualized learning takes place. Lindvall (1967) has 14 categories for independent work which include such individual activities as reading, watching a film-strip, listening to a tape, checking work, taking an individual test and completing a work-sheet. His system also has a number of categories for non-instructional use of pupil time like 'waiting for materials', 'going to fetch material' and 'waiting to talk to the teacher'. When students are working with project groups or in workshop situations this could be a very useful instrument for describing the behaviour of the children in their classes.

Honigman and Stephens (1969) designed their system to include use of hardware materials, such as cassettes, games or slide projectors; reading activities; writing activities; interaction between children, including both task-relevant and social talk; interaction with the teacher and positive learning, i.e. watching or listening. This seems again a very useful system for describing lessons when children are not being taught as a whole class but are learning on their own or in small groups. The hardware aspect may, at the moment, be more relevant to individualized learning as understood in the United States, but the system generally could easily be used in less formal situations here.

(b) Some theoretical considerations
(i) *Flexibility*

Variable 51 in this research, the so-called Flexibility Factor is a measure of variety within the terms of the Flanders system. As a measure of variety of teaching pattern it merits closer scrutiny. Details of its calculation are given in the Appendix.

Two examples are given below in Table 15 of contrasting types of Mathematics teacher. Student teacher A chose a lecturing style in every one of the four lessons given in the Table, as shown both by the lesson reports, and a range of 72 per cent to 89 per cent was recorded in category five (lecture). Because of this, the lecture category is always large and the other categories correspondingly small. The flexibility factor of Student A was 16, among the lowest recorded. Student B, another mathematician, had a varied lesson pattern in terms of the ten categories. In the first lesson she made extensive use of question and answer, and a similar pattern is seen in her fourth lesson, though with more lecture. Her second lesson was more of a workshop, after a lecture and question and answer introduction, but her third lesson consisted almost entirely of children working out problems from a duplicated sheet she had distributed. Her flexibility factor is 52, much higher than Student A, but not among the highest recorded in the sample.

Contrary to the findings of Flanders (1967), who used i/d ratios from several lessons as measures of flexibility of teaching pattern, there was no association in the present research between the flexibility factor and the various measures of effectiveness.

There was a tendency for students teaching certain subjects to have very high or very low flexibility factors. An analysis of the FF scores by individual students according to main subject specialism gave the following mean FF scores.

English	64	Geography	38	Languages	32
Art	42	Chemistry	37	Biology	30
History	42	Maths	33	Physics	28

Table 15: *Comparison of the flexibility factors of two Mathematics students*

Cat.	Lesson				Cat.	Lesson			
	1st	2nd	3rd	4th		1st	2nd	3rd	4th
1	0	0	0	0	1	0	0	0	0
2	0	0	2	0	2	8	0	0	4
3	0	0	1	0	3	2	4	0	4
4	7	4	6	1	4	21	10	2	13
5	72	82	80	89	5	11	24	6	21
6	7	4	0	1	6	3	2	0	5
7	0	0	0	0	7	0	2	0	2
8	6	2	2	2	8	17	6	1	15
9	2	1	1	2	9	4	5	2	4
10	6	7	8	5	10	34	47	89	32
Total	100	100	100	100	Total	100	100	100	100

Student A (FF = 16)   *Student B (FF = 52)*

This underlines the subjective lesson reporting by the observers that English teachers tended to have varied lesson patterns, whereas Languages and Science tended to be more stereotyped.

Finally, one needs to consider whether the flexibility factors are low generally, i.e., whether most students tend to use a limited range of strategies as measured by the Flanders system. This is difficult to decide because (a) there are no published norms, nor can there be unless conditions are made similar, and (b) in any case little research has been conducted in the area.

It was decided, however, to compare the mean flexibility factor of the whole group (FF $=39\cdot6$) with a figure derived as follows. A table of random numbers was used to assemble ten imaginary students by taking a first lesson from among all the first lessons observed, a second lesson from all the second lessons and so on until ten randomly chosen sets of four lessons had been assembled. The FF of each of the ten ranged from 53 to 75 with a mean of $60\cdot2$ compared with the mean of $39\cdot5$ for the whole group. The difference between these two means was shown by a t-test to be significant at greater than the one per cent level of confidence. This would tentatively suggest that most students have a relatively stable personal lesson pattern, especially in Languages and Science, when compared with a random choice of lessons from different students.

(ii) *Teaching styles*

The cluster analysis as well as flow chart analysis of subject matrices showed certain common strategies in use. Seven micro-paradigms can be constructed from chains of Flanders categories frequently observed.

1. *Continuous lecture* occasionally punctuated by silence gives a sequence of 5–5–5–5–10–5–5–5–5–10 which was frequently observed in Geography lessons and was a part of most lessons.

2. *Reinforced high-speed drill* consisted of a question-answer-praise sequence and was frequently noted in the foreign language parts of modern language lessons or when teachers were testing. The sequence of 4–8–2–4–8–2 is repeated.

3. *Programmed instruction* uses the sequence 5–5–4–8–3–2–5–5, showing the 'frame' of information followed by question, answer, acceptance, praise and further information. It was used extensively by some Geography and History teachers and was more common in the Lower and Middle School rather than in the Upper School.

4. *Directive style* centred around the 6–6 cell and was common in Science lessons, especially Biology, certain types of Language lessons and with younger age-groups. The sequence was 6–6–10–10–6–8–10–10.

5. *Disorder* often manifested itself as strings of category ten representing chaos rather than silence and category seven. It was rare in girls' schools and the Upper Schools. Category nine occurred when children called out, giving a sequence such as 10–10–7–7–7–9 –7–10–7.

Pupil-oriented discussion had its focus around the 9–9 cell and tended to be most common in English and History lessons and with the youngest and oldest age groups. It was commonly observed after half-term, possibly because students then felt able to act as non-directive chairmen. It rarely occurred in Science or Language lessons. The sequence was 9–9–9–9–1–9–9–9–3–9–9–5–9–9.

7. *Workshop* produced a heavily tallied 10–10 cell as children worked in pairs or small groups. The teacher tended to service the groups, going round asking questions. The Flanders system is not entirely adequate to describe this kind of activity. Science and Maths lessons regularly produced a sequence like 10–10–10–9–5–9–5–10–10–10–4–8–4–8–8–10–10.

(c) **Some practical considerations**
(i) *Training teachers*

If students tend to use a limited range of teaching tactics, as suggested above, there is a case for considering ways of affecting their behaviour in the classroom to widen the range of strategies at their disposal.

A controlled experiment with 16 students (Wragg, 1971) showed that students who saw a combination of videotape and interaction analysis categories after the teach lesson of a micro-teaching format, were more likely to be rated higher by the children on the re-teach and to change their interaction pattern than those receiving videotape or inter-action analysis feedback only or no feedback at all.

The disadvantage of carrying out research under controlled conditions outside the school environment is that the conditions are only partially realistic. The children and teacher are not necessarily too different from what they would be in school, but changes shown to occur in these conditions might not occur in the long term. For example, it is relatively easy for a student to praise more frequently in a re-teach lesson, but this does not necessarily mean he will make extensive use of praise once he starts teaching.

It was noteworthy that, in the pilot year, the mean use of category one, acceptance of feelings, was six tallies per thousand as opposed to less than one tally per thousand in the main 1969/70 study; that use of category three, acceptance of ideas, increased from 22 tallies per thousand in the early stages to 30 tallies per thousand in the late stages; that use of category nine, unsolicited pupil talk, went up from 20 tallies per thousand in the first period to 87 tallies per thousand in the final phase, that pupil talk generally increased from 149 tallies per thousand in the first period to 210 tallies per thousand in the final period. None of these trends was noted in the main study, when, of course, there was no feedback of information to the students being observed, and it must be regarded as a strong possibility that they occurred as a result of feedback. If this were so, it would suggest that regular feedback of interaction data can make students more aware of their teaching pattern, increase the occurrence of pupil talk, and also increase the likelihood of students accepting the children's ideas and feelings.

(ii) *Future research*

There is a clear need for further research into the classroom behaviour of student teach-ers. Future studies could concern themselves with home background and classroom style. Do students from working class backgrounds interact "better" with working class children ?

School background too might be considered. It is well known that past models can powerfully influence students' teaching styles yet little is known about how this happens.

Preparation for teaching is also a factor to be investigated. Flanders (1963) wrote.

'It is a serious indictment of the profession, however, to hear so many education instructors say that their students will appreciate what they are learning *after* they have had some practical teaching experience. What hurts is the obvious hypocrisy of making the statement and then giving a lecture on the importance of presenting material in such a way that the immediate needs and interests of the pupils are taken into consideration. Such instances reveal a misunderstanding of theory and practice. To be understood, concepts in education must be verified by personal field experience, in turn field experiences must be efficiently conceptualized to gain insight. With most present practices, the gorge between theory and practice grows deeper and wider, excavated by the very individuals who are pledged to fill it.'

It is not easy to identify the real effects of various kinds of training on eventual classroom behaviour. A single lecture, a group discussion, a film, a series of meetings, the influence of fellow students, the influences of a tutor, all these may affect the classroom behaviour of a student to a greater or lesser degree. Even without the support of research findings one would expect that some tutors powerfully shape the classroom behaviour of their students.

Also worthy of study are the effects of different classes on students' teaching, as well as the effects of room layout and design and equipment.

(iii) *Replication studies*

Several important points must be made about the findings of this research and their interpretation both for the ordinary reader and the researcher wishing to replicate or modify the research.

1. At the time of the research, graduate training was not compulsory. Future investigators may be looking at groups which are no longer entirely 'voluntary', in that they may contain a small number of students who might have preferred to enter teaching immediately after graduating.

2. The South West of England covers a wide area with a mixture of rural and urban schools. Many University Departments place their students predominantly in urban schools.

3. As is the case with all other Departments the UDE at Exeter in unique. Its staff, its facilities, its students, the schools it uses, its teaching techniques are all unique. It may be similar to other University Departments but it is also essentially different. Even a replication study within the same Department the following year should produce some differences due to differences in student preparation, change of climate in schools, difference in students' personalities, however small these might be.

4. At the time of the present research, most South-West secondary schools had not been reorganized. As time proceeds more graduate students are likely to be doing their teaching practice in non-selective schools and possibly in unstreamed classes. This could lead to significant differences in the interaction patterns observed.

Given these and other important differences, there is still a need for at least one other study of a similar nature in another College or Department where graduates are being trained, as well as a pressing need for non-graduate students in primary schools to be studied. It is quite possible that very different observation instruments will need to be designed for observing students in primary schools, but the absence of a large-scale descriptive study in this area leaves an important gap in the research literature.

IV SUMMARY

Analysis of published research in the area of teacher education showed that there was no major British study of the classroom behaviour of student teachers during teaching practice based on live observation.

After a pilot study in 1968/69, in which data on almost 100 lessons given by over 30 students were analysed, the main study examined the classroom behaviour of 102 graduate student teachers in 41 schools. A team of six observers was trained to use the Flanders system of interaction analysis until high levels of inter-observer agreement were obtained. They then collected data on 578 lessons given by the 102 students.

Data analysis was performed using the Exeter University computer, and separate millage matrices were compiled for men and women teachers, subject being taught, age and sex grouping of classes, and stage of teaching practice at which lesson was given.

In addition the live observation data were related to measures of personality, values, creativity, intelligence, attainment and ratings of effectiveness. A number of relationships between presage and process variables were shown to exist, and analysis of variance was used to examine differences between groups of students rated above average and below average in teaching competence by supervising tutors and Heads of schools. Few positive links were found between measures of effectiveness and other variables.

A factor analysis was performed on 39 of the variables and 14 factors emerged. A cluster analysis of the classroom variables showed that, although teachers of English adopted varying patterns, teachers of other subjects, especially Language and Science, tended to have similar patterns to each other. From these analyses and inspection of the 578 individual matrices, a number of micro-paradigms of teaching behaviour were constructed. Many students were shown to have fixed and predictable patterns, and subject being taught exercised greatest influence on classroom interaction.

Finally there was an exploration of certain areas where further research appeared to be needed, as well as a consideration of the practical and theoretical importance of the findings of the present inquiry.

BIBLIOGRAPHY

ADAMS, R. S. and BIDDLE, B. J. (1970). *Realities of Teaching*. New York: Holt, Rinehart and Winston.

ALLEN, E. A. (1963). 'The professional training of teachers', *Educ. Res.*, **5**, 3, 200–15.

ALTMAN, H. (1969). *A Science Observation System*. Los Angeles: University of California.

AMIDON, E. J. and FLANDERS, N. A. (1961). 'The effects of direct and indirect teacher influence on dependent-prone students learning geometry', *J. Educ. Psychol.*, **52**, 286–91.

AMIDON, E. J. and FLANDERS, N. A. (1963). *The Role of the Teacher in the Classroom*. Minnesota: Paul S. Amidon and Associates Inc.

AMIDON, E. J. and GIAMMATTEO, M. (1965). 'The verbal behaviour of superior elementary school teachers', *Elementary School J.*, **65**, 283–5.

AMIDON, E. J. and HOUGH, J. B. (1967). *Interaction Analysis—Theory, Research and Application*. Reading, Mass.: Addison-Wesley.

ANDERSON, H. H. (1939). 'The measurement of domination and of socially integrative behaviour in teachers' contacts with children', *Child Development*, **10**, 73–89.

ANDERSON, H. H. and BREWER, J. E. (1945). *Studies of Teachers' Classroom Personalities*. Psychological Monographs No. 6.

ASHLEY, B., COHEN, H. and SLATTER, R. (1967). 'Social classifications: relevance to the teacher', *Times Educ. Suppl.* March 17.

BARR, A. S. (1961). 'Wisconsin studies of the measurement and prediction of teacher effectiveness: a summary of investigations', *J. Exp. Educ.*, **30**, 5–156.

BELLACK, A. A., KLIEBARD, H. M., HYMAN, R. T. and SMITH, F. L. (1966). *The Language of the Classroom*. Columbia: Teacher's College Press.

BEREDAY, G. Z. F. and LAUWERYS, J. A. (Eds.) (1963). 'The Education and Training of Teachers'. In: *The Yearbook of Education 1963*. London: Evans.

BUTCHER, H. J. (1965). 'The attitudes of student teachers to education: a comparison with the attitudes of experienced teachers and a study of changes during the training course', *Brit. J. Soc. & Clin. Psych.*, 4, 17–24.

CANE, B. (1968). *Research into Teacher Education*. Slough: NFER.

CANE, B. (1968). 'Teachers, Teaching and Teacher Education'. In: BUTCHER, H. J. (Ed.) *Educational Research in Britain*. London: University of London Press.

CATTELL, R. B. (1970). *The Scientific Analysis of Personality*. London: Pelican.

CLEMENTS, R. D. (1967). 'Art teacher—student questioning and dialogue in the classroom', *Classroom Interaction Newsletter*, 2, 22–3.

COGAN, M. L. (1956). 'Theory and design of a study of teacher-pupil interaction', *Harvard Educ. Rev.*, 26, 315–42.

COOK, W. W. and LEEDS, C. H. (1947). 'Measuring the teaching personality', *Educ. & Psychol. Measmt.*, 7, 399–410.

COPE, E. (1970). 'Teacher training and school practice', *Educ. Res.*, 12, 2, 87–98.

CORTIS, G. A. (1968). 'Predicting student performance in colleges of education', *Brit. J. Educ. Psychol.*, 38, 2, 115–22.

DAVIES, L. S. (1961). 'Some relationships between attitudes, personality, characteristics, and verbal behaviour of selected teachers'. Unpublished PhD thesis, University of Minnesota.

ERICKSON, H. E. (1954). 'A factorial study of teaching ability', *J. Exp. Educ.*, 23, 1–39.

EVANS, D. and WRAGG, E. C. (1969). 'The use of a verbal interaction analysis technique with severely subnormal children', *J. Mental Subnormality*.

EVANS, E. G. S. (1964). 'Reasoning ability and personality differences amongst student teachers', *Brit. J. Educ. Psychol.*, 34, 305–14.

EVANS, K. M. (1951). 'A critical survey of methods of assessing teacher ability', *Brit. J. Educ. Psychol.*, 21, 2, 89–95.

EVANS, K. M. (1952). 'A study of attitude towards teaching as a career', *Brit. J. Educ. Psychol.*, 22, 1, 63–9.

EVANS, K. M. (1957). 'Is the concept of "interest" of significance to success in a teacher training course?' *Educ. Rev.*, 9, 205–11.

EVANS, K. M. (1958). 'An examination of the Minnesota Teacher Attitude Inventory', *Brit. J. Educ. Psychol.*, 28, 3, 253–57.

EVANS, K. M. (1961). 'An annotated bibliography of British research on teaching and teaching ability', *Educ. Res.*, 4, 1, 67–80.

EVANS, K. M. (1966). 'The Minnesota Teacher Attitude Inventory', *Educ. Res.*, 8, 134–41.

EVANS, K. M. (1968). 'Teacher training courses and students' personal qualities', *Educ. Res.*, 10, 1, 72–7.

FLANDERS, N. A. (1960). 'Interaction Analysis in the classroom: A Manual for Observers'. (Mimeographed). University of Minnesota.

FLANDERS, N. A. (1962). 'A Cross-National Comparison of New Zealand and Minnesota Teacher–Pupil Relations'. Paper read at AERA convention, Atlantic City.

FLANDERS, N. A. (1963). 'Intent, action and feedback: a preparation for teaching', *J. Teacher Educ.*, 14, 251–60.

FLANDERS, N. A. (1965). 'Teacher influence, Pupil Attitudes and Achievement', US Department of Health, Education and Welfare co-operative research monograph, No. 12.

FLANDERS, N. A. (1967). 'Teacher Influence in the Classroom'. In: AMIDON, E. J. and HOUGH, J. B., *Interaction Analysis*. Reading, Mass.: Addison-Wesley.

FLANDERS, N. A. (1970). *Analysing Classroom Behaviour*. New York: Addison-Wesley.

FURST, N. A. (1967). 'The multiple language of the classroom: a further analysis and a synthesis of meanings communicated in High School teaching'. Unpublished PhD thesis, Temple University.

FURST, N. A. (1967). 'The effects of training in interaction analysis on the behaviour of student teachers in secondary schools'. In: AMIDON, E. J. and HOUGH, J. B., *Interaction Analysis*. Reading, Mass.: Addison-Wesley.

GAGE, N. L. (Ed.) (1963). *Handbook of Research on Teaching*. Chicago: American Educational Research Association, Rand McNally.

HADLEY, S. T. (1954). 'A study of the predictive value of several variables to student teaching success as measured by student teaching marks', *Teachers' College Bulletin*, 60, 1–10.

HALLWORTH, H. J. (1965). *A System of Computer Programs for Use in Psychology and Education*. London: Brit. Psych. Soc. Publications.

HEIM, A. W. (1968). *AH5 Group Test of High Grade Intelligence* (Manual). Slough: NFER.

HERBERT, N. and TURNBULL, G. H. (1963). 'Personality factors and effective progress in teaching', *Educ. Rev.*, **16**, 24–31.

HONIGMAN, F. K. and STEPHENS, J. (1969). *Analysing student functioning in an Individualized Instructional Setting*. Fort Lauderdale, Florida: Nea Rad Inc.

HOUGH, J. B. (1966). 'An observational system for the analysis of classroom instruction'. Unpublished paper, Ohio State University, Columbia.

HOUGH, J. B. and AMIDON, E. J. (1963). 'Behavioural change in pre-service teacher preparation; an experimental study'. Unpublished paper, Temple University.

HUNTER, E. (1968). 'The Effect of Training in the Use of New Science Programs upon the classroom verbal behaviour of First Grade Teachers as they teach science'. Hunter College, New York.

KOERNER, J. D. (1965). *The Miseducation of American Teachers*. Baltimore: Pelican.

LEWIN, K., LIPPITT, R. and WHITE, R. K. (1939). 'Patterns of aggressive behaviour in experimentally created "social climates",' *J. Soc. Psychol.*, **10**, 271–99.

LINDVALL, C. M. (1967). 'The role of classroom observation in the improvement of instruction', *Classroom Interaction Newsletter*, **3**, 16–19.

MANN, J. F. (1961). 'An investigation into the various factors influencing success in completing a course in teacher training'. Unpublished PhD thesis. London University.

MATHER, P. M. (1969). 'Computer applications in the Natural and Social Sciences, No. 1: Cluster Analysis'. Nottingham University.

MATTHEWS, C. C. (1969). 'Child-structured learning in Science: a research and development project of the Department of Science Education'. Florida State University, Tallahassee.

MORRISON, A. and McINTYRE, D. (1969). *Teachers and Teaching*. London: Penguin.

MOSKOWITZ, G. (1966). *The Flint System: An Observational Tool for the Foreign Language Class*. Philadelphia: Temple University.

MOSKOWITZ, G. (1967). 'The Attitudes and Teaching Patterns of Co-operating Teachers and Student Teachers Trained in Interaction Analysis'. In: AMIDON, E. J. and HOUGH, J. B., *Interaction Analysis*. Reading, Mass.: Addison-Wesley.

NATIONAL UNION OF TEACHERS (1970). *Teacher Education—the Way Ahead*. London: NUT.

PANCRATZ, R. (1967). 'Verbal Interaction Patterns in the classrooms of selected Physics teachers'. In: AMIDON, E. J. and HOUGH, J. B., *Interaction Analysis*. Reading, Mass.: Addison-Wesley.

PARAKH, J. S. (1967). 'A study of the relationships among teacher behaviour, pupil behaviour, and pupil characteristics in high school Biology classes'. Western Washington State College, Bellingham.

PEDLEY, R. (1969). 'The Comprehensive University', Inaugural Lecture, Exeter University.

PERKINS, H. V. (1965). 'Classroom behaviour and under-achievement', *Amer. Educ. Res. J.*, **2**, 1–12.

POPPLETON, P. K. (1968). 'The assessment of teaching practice. What criteria do we use?' *Education for Teaching*, **75**, 59–64.

POWELL, E. R. (1968). 'Teacher behaviour and pupil achievement', *Classroom Interaction Newsletter*, **3**, 3, 23.

ROGERS, C. W. (1966). 'The interpersonal relationship in the facilitation of learning'. Lecture at Harvard. Mimeograph.

ROSENSHINE, B. (1969). 'Teaching behaviours related to pupil achievement', *Classroom Interaction Newsletter*, **5**, 1.

SCHUELER, H., GOLD, M. J. and MITZEL, H. E. (1962). 'The use of television for improving teacher training and for improving measures of student-teaching performance'. City University, New York.

SCOTT, M. V. (1955). 'Reliability of content analysis: the case of nominal coding', *Public Opinion Quarterly*, **19**, 321–25.

SEAGOE, M. V. (1946). 'Prediction of in-service success in teaching', *J. Educ. Res.*, **39**, 658–63.

SIMON, A. and BOYER, E. G. (Ed.) (1968). *Mirrors for Behaviour* (Vols. 1 to 6). Philadelphia: Research for Better Schools Inc.

SIMON, A. and BOYER, E. G. (Ed.) (1970). *Mirrors for Behaviour* (Vols. 7 to 14 and summary). Philadelphia: Research for Better Schools Inc.

SPAULDING, R. L. (1965). 'Achievement, creativity and self-concept correlates of teacher–pupil transactions in elementary schools'. US Office of Education Co-operative Research Project No. 1352.

SPROULE, A. (1970). 'Colleges slated by NFER in shock report on training', *Times Educ. Suppl.*, February 13.

START, K. B. (1966). 'The relationship of teaching ability to measures of personality', *Brit. J. Educ. Psychol.*, **36**, 158–65.

STEVENS, R. (1912). *The Question as a Measure of Efficiency in Instruction: a Critical Study of Classroom Practice*. Columbia: Teachers College Press.

STONE, J. C. (1968). *Breakthrough in Teacher Education*. San Francisco: Jossey-Bass Inc.

TANNER, W. C. (1954). 'Personality bases in teacher selection', *Phi. Delta Kappa*, **35**, 271–77.

TORRANCE, E. P. (1966). *Torrance Tests of Creative Thinking*. New Jersey: Personnel Press Inc.

UNIVERSITY OF TOLEDO. (1965). *The Characteristics of Teacher Education Students in the British Isles and the United States*. Ohio: Research Foundation of the University of Toledo.

WARBURTON, F. W., BUTCHER, H. J. and FORREST, G. M. (1963). 'Predicting student performance in a University Department of Education', *Brit. J. Educ. Psychol.*, **23**, 68–79.

WEBER, W. A. (1968). 'Teacher behaviour and pupil creativity', *Classroom Interaction Newsletter*, **3**, 3, 30.

WISEMAN, S. (1963). 'Assessing the ability of experienced teachers', *Advancement of Science*, May, 1963, 57–64.

WITHALL, J. (1949). 'The development of a technique for the measurement of social-emotional climate in classrooms', *J. Exp. Educ.*, **17**, 347–61.

WRAGG, E. C. (1967). 'Attitudes, anxieties and aspirations of graduates following the postgraduate certificate of education'. Unpublished MEd thesis, Leicester University.

WRAGG, E. C. (1968). 'Closed-circuit television and the training of teachers', *Times Educ. Suppl.*, July 19.

WRAGG, E. C. (1970a). 'Practical training for graduates', *Times Educ. Suppl.*, February 5.

WRAGG, E. C. (1970b). 'Interaction analysis as a feedback system for student teachers', *Education for Teaching*, Spring 1970.

WRAGG, E. C. (1970c). 'Interaction analysis in the foreign language classroom', *Modern Language J.*, February 1970.

WRAGG, E. C. (1970d). 'Identifying individual responses during classroom interaction', *Classroom Interaction Newsletter*, **5**, 2.

WRAGG, E. C. (1971). 'The influence of feedback on teachers' performance', *Educ. Res.*, **13**, 3, 218–21.

WRAGG, E. C. (1972). 'An analysis of the verbal classroom interaction between graduate student teachers and children'. Unpublished PhD thesis, Exeter University.

WRIGHT, E. M. J. (1966). 'Interaction Analysis to study pupil involvement and mathematical content', *Classroom Interaction Newsletter*, **2**, 5.

ZAHN, R. D. (1965). 'The use of interaction analysis in supervising student teachers'. Unpublished PhD thesis, Temple University.

APPENDIX

Summary of the 54 variables

The 28 presage variables, 23 process variables, and 3 product variables are now given below in numerical order:

Presage variables
(1) Cattell 16 PF, Factor A
(2)   ,,   ,,   Factor B
(3)   ,,   ,,   Factor C
(4)   ,,   ,,   Factor E
(5)   ,,   ,,   Factor F
(6)   ,,   ,,   Factor G
(7)   ,,   ,,   Factor H

(8)	„	„	Factor I
(9)	„	„	Factor L
(10)	„	„	Factor M
(11)	„	„	Factor N
(12)	„	„	Factor O
(13)	„	„	Factor Q1
(14)	„	„	Factor Q2
(15)	„	„	Factor Q3
(16)	„	„	Factor Q4

(17) Allport-Vernon-Lindzey Study of Values—Theoretical
(18) „ „ „ „ „ —Economic
(19) „ „ „ „ „ —Aesthetic
(20) „ „ „ „ „ —Social
(21) „ „ „ „ „ —Political
(22) „ „ „ „ „ —Religious
(23) Torrance Tests of Creative Thinking—(Verbal Test B)—Fluency Score
(24) „ „ „ „ „ „ —Flexibility Score
(25) „ „ „ „ „ „ —Originality Score
(26) „ „ „ „ „ „ —Total of all 3 scores
(27) Alice Heim AH5 High-grade intelligence test score.
(28) Degree Class

Process Variables (all based on Flanders system)
(29) Tallies per thousand in category 1
(30) „ „ „ „ 2
(31) „ „ „ „ 3
(32) „ „ „ „ 4
(33) „ „ „ „ 5
(34) „ „ „ „ 6
(35) „ „ „ „ 7
(36) „ „ „ „ 8
(37) „ „ „ „ 9
(38) „ „ „ „ 10
(39) Percentage of talk in the lesson
(40) Percentage of talk by the teacher
(41) I/D ratio
(42) i/d ratio
(43) Teacher Response Ratio (TRR)
(44) Teacher Question Ratio (TQR)
(45) Pupil Initiation Ratio (PIR)
(46) Instantaneous Teacher Response Ratio (TRR 8/9)
(47) Instantaneous Teacher Question Ratio (TQR 8/9)
(48) Content Cross Ratio (CCR)
(49) Steady State Ratio (SSR)
(50) Pupil Steady State Ratio (PSSR)
(51) Flexibility Factor (FF)

Product variables
(52) Teaching practice school rating
(53) Supervising tutor's rating
(54) School's and tutor's ratings combined

The Flexibility Factor (FF), variable 51, was calculated according to a suggestion made by Flanders (1970). It is an attempt to get some measure of students whose patterns for different lessons are very similar as measured by the Flanders technique, as compared with those who show a very varied pattern. It is a rather more complex calculation than the other process variables. It is calculated by taking the first four lessons given by every student (four lessons because every student was watched at least four times). The next stage is to calculate the category totals for each lesson as a percentage figure. The percentages of each category are taken category by category and the standard deviation is calculated of the four lessons for that category. Finally the ten standard deviations are summed to gived the Flexibility Factor (FF). The principle behind this is that a student who gave four nearly identical lessons in terms of distribution of talk, such as, for example, always between two per cent and three per cent praise, between 33 per cent and 35 per cent lecture, and so on, will produce small standard deviation scores and these will total to give a small FF. On the other hand the student who varies widely, say from two per cent to eight per cent praise, 15 per cent to 50 per cent lecture etc., will produce ten much larger standard deviations and hence a much larger FF. This factor has never been used in reported research to the writer's knowledge, nor are there any published norms, since, clearly, these are impossible to establish other than where conditions of observation and number of lessons observed are identical.

Teacher Self-Concept and Teaching Style

Norma Trowbridge
George Mason College
of the University of Virginia, USA

Though general reasoning suggests that there should be a relationship between a teacher's attitudes, opinions and perceptions of herself and her style of teaching, little empirical evidence about such relationships has been published.

This study attempts to analyse data obtained in a longitudinal four-year investigation carried out under a Title III project of Public Law 89–10, Elementary and Secondary Act.[1] Although these data were originally collected for other purposes, they were found to lend themselves to the study of the relation between how a teacher perceives herself and the way she teaches.

In most correlation studies the major difficulties lie in good quantitative measures of the factors under study.

Measurement of a teacher's self-concept was found to be not too difficult, because a satisfactory measure, based on self-inventory, has been developed. Measurement of teaching style was more difficult and presented crucial problems. Indeed, a fully satisfactory measure of the various factors that make up the concept of 'teaching style' is not likely to be found.

Obviously, it is more desirable to assess teaching style by a teacher's performance in a classroom than by a paper and pencil test. Verbal interaction techniques make such a procedure feasible. A number of aspects of teaching style have been studied by this method. The specific dimension explored in this investigation was the kinds of thinking processes used by the teacher which in turn highly determine the kinds of thinking processes used by the students (Gallagher, 1960; Trowbridge, 1970).

Purposes

The purposes of the study were to determine:

(1) the extent of differences in teacher self-concept,

(2) the relation between teacher self-concept and the kinds of thinking teachers use,

(3) the relation between teacher self-concept and the amount of time spent in non-thinking activities,

[1]Project was funded under Title III, Public Law 89–10, Elementary and Secondary Education Act of 1965, Grant No. OEG–3–7–703575–5055; as well as Grant No. OEG–0–9–254064–1820–725 under the Education Professions Development Act (EPDA). The author wishes to express appreciation for the assistance and co-operation of the staff of the project, especially Drs Bill Clark, Joe Millard and Marl Ramsay; Helen Coe, Rita BeLieu and Shirley Whitaker. The author is also grateful for four years of support and sincere interest from the Polk County Board of Education and Dr Ralph Norris, County Superintendent of Schools.

(4) the relation between teacher self-concept and the amount of time teachers allow to talk, and

(5) any possible difference between elementary and secondary teachers.

Measurement of self-concept

Self-concept research presents, as Wylie (1961, page 62) explained, a 'bewildering array' of definitions, hypotheses, criteria, testing instruments, sample groups and research methods. Therefore pilot study attempts using different instruments and techniques were carried out.

Eventually the *Tennessee Self-Concept Scale* (Fitts, 1965) was used as the instrument to measure self-concept of teachers. It was chosen largely because of its wide use and the relatively large number of studies available providing normative data.

The *Tennessee Self-Concept Scale* is a 100-item self-reporting instrument on which the person being measured indicates the way he perceives himself on a five-position scale. Although the items are arranged in several sub-tests, the total self-concept score was accepted as indicating the teacher's self-concept. The *Tennessee Self-Concept Scale* is probably as good an instrument for measuring adults' self-concepts as has so far been devised; it has been widely used and studied in many research investigations as well as in clinical and school settings.

Items on the *Tennessee Self-Concept Scale* deal with such things as whether the subject likes to look nice and neat, whether he regards himself as religious, whether he has a lot of self-control, whether he sees himself as hateful, whether he believes that his friends have confidence in him, whether he frequently changes his mind, and so on.

The mean self-concept score of teachers in the study was 352·16, slightly higher than the mean reported in the normative studies in the manual, 345·57. The range was from 201 to 392 with a standard deviation of 24·72. These data essentially substantiate Fitts' data.

Measurement of one aspect of teaching style-thinking processes

The measurement of thinking processes presents numerous problems, the most critical ones being: (1) a theoretical framework to provide a structure for examination of thinking; (2) definition of various thinking operations or categories; and (3) criteria for measuring them. After investigation of several theoretical systems for analysing thought processes (Bloom, 1965; Guilford, 1956; Piaget, 1951), J. P. Guilford's conceptual definition of thinking operations, as defined in his model of the Structure of Intellect, was chosen to provide (1) theoretical framework and (2) definitions of various thinking operations. This was coupled with a measurement instrument specifically designed by Mary Jane Aschner and James Gallagher (1962) to provide (3) operational criteria for Guilford's classifications and a measurement technique for assessing them.

In Guilford's model of the Structure of Intellect he describes five classes of thinking operations. 'Memory,' 'cognition,' 'convergent-thinking,' 'divergent-thinking.' and 'evaluative-thinking,' according to Guilford, are five broad categories under which all thinking activity can be placed (Guilford, 1956).

Guilford's five general classifications of thinking processes are defined as follows:

(1) memory—simple recall or retrieval of information

(2) cognition—recognition or knowing, simple understanding

(3) convergent—thinking processes involving use of memory and cognition as well as analysis and integration of data and experience, generally designed to arrive at one expected result.

(4) divergent-thinking processes usually designated as 'creative thinking,' such as originality, flexibility, fluency, elaboration, and synthesis, in which there may be multiple appropriate responses.

(5) evaluative—thought processes involving value rather than facts or data, and concerning thinking of a judgmental nature. At times the person uses a given value dimension; at other times he must construct his own value dimension and subsequently judge something according to the scale.

Because there is always time in every classroom when no thinking process is occurring (at least none that can be measured by verbal interaction methods), a category for non-thinking activity was developed and labelled 'routine'. Activities occurring in classrooms which fall in this category are procedures like taking roll, getting lunch money, lining up in rows, passing out paper, books, art materials, etc. It also includes time spent with admonitions such as 'Settle down now . . . and one of us isn't ready yet . . .' or 'Mary, we are waiting . . .; we are all waiting for Mary . . .'

The Aschner-Gallagher instrument is a 'verbal interaction analysis' technique which was designed for the express purpose of measuring the amounts of the Guilford thinking processes actually occurring in a given classroom. A random sample of classroom time is selected and a trained observer records at 15-second intervals the type of thinking being expressed in the talking that is going on (i.e., the verbal interaction). The eventual product of the analysis is a statistical distribution of classroom time among the Guilford thinking-process classifications.

A sample of such a distribution might appear as follows:

Percentage of time spent in Guilford's thinking processes

	Memory and Cognition	Convergent	Divergent	Evaluative	Routine
Teacher A	19·2%	21·4%	10·8%	10·3%	38·3%
Teacher B	18·4%	24·5%	8·1%	9·8%	39·2%

Any number of samples of classroom activity can be used; data from the samples of a teacher can be averaged to provide a description over time of the thinking behaviour of her classroom.

There are some details of the operation of the Aschner-Gallagher method which should be noted. First, since it is nearly impossible to distinguish between Guilford's 'cognition' and 'memory' categories by listening to a verbal exchange, these two are combined on the Aschner-Gallagher scale. Second, in addition to the Guilford thinking processes, the analysis measures the percentage of time in the random sample in which the students were talking (and the teacher was not). Finally, there is the category mentioned earlier called 'routine', in which the analyst places his tallies when non-thinking (house-keeping and student management) needs are being attended to in the classroom and no observable thinking operations are taking place.

The investigation's adaptation of the Aschner-Gallagher technique involved the use of audio-tape-recordings (both video-tape-recording and direct-observation methods were tried, but dropped because both intruded too forcefully upon the normal classroom activity). Each sample consisted of a full hour of taped classroom conversation, but the 15-second tallies were performed only on three 10-minute periods selected at random on each tape. A 10-minute period was extended as necessary if part of the conversation was unintelligible so that a full 10 minutes of interaction would be tallied. An average of five tapes from a given classroom during a year was assumed to provide a reasonably representative sample of the thinking activities typically occurring in it.

Problems with analyst training, inter-analyst reliability (i.e., ensuring that all analysts had very similar judgment in tallying the thinking operations), teacher co-operation and other practical difficulties were found to be surmountable.

Procedure

Audio-tape samples of classroom behaviour were collected from the classroom of each teacher in the sample in accordance with the A-G manual. On the average, five one-hour taped samples were collected per teacher per year. Since teachers were followed for more than one year, and since secondary teachers shift from one class to another throughout the day, the samples for a given teacher involved more than one group of students.

The *Tennessee Self-Concept Scale* was administered to the teachers under conditions designed to encourage careful and honest response to each item. Anonymity was carefully preserved, and each teacher was given an opportunity for a personal interpretation of the self-concept scale if desired. In addition, the fact that these teachers were co-operative enough to make available tape-recordings of their classroom activities, encouraged the belief they would be conscientious in filling out the self-concept inventory.

Sample

The sample consisted of 302 elementary teachers and 56 secondary teachers from central United States, with the largest number coming from central Iowa. Since the procedures were amenable to use with all ages of children, classrooms representing first through twelfth grade were included. The classrooms in the sample represent a diversity of income groups, ethnic backgrounds, city and country schools and races.

Results

The data of the study were statistically analysed to provide results relative to the relationships between a teacher's self-concept and the percentage of classroom time:

(1) she talks;
(2) she spends on routine;
(3) she uses various thinking processes.

In the Aschner-Gallagher interaction technique teacher-talk is tallied separately from student-talk. Therefore, data were available for correlation between a teacher's self-concept and the proportion of classroom time she talks. The overall resulting correlation coefficient was −·624.

To demonstrate this relationship more clearly, teachers were divided into two equal groups, the half with lower self-concepts and the half with higher self-concepts. Figure 1 displays the results.

It can readily be seen that the teachers with lower self-concepts talk more, and therefore allow their students to talk less. In the two groups the percentages were almost reversed.

The second analysis was concerned with the amount of classroom time spent in routine. In earlier extensive investigations (Clark and Trowbridge, 1971; Trowbridge, 1969, 1970) it was found that the average amount of time the teacher spent on routine was about 39 per cent–40 per cent of the classroom day. This proportion was fairly consistent over all samples.

To determine what relationship might exist between teacher self-concept and the amount of time spent on routine, a correlation was run between the teacher's self-concept score and the proportion of routine shown on all her audio-tapes. The resulting overall correlation coefficient was –·383. Dividing the teachers as before into the upper and lower self-concept groups, it was found that teachers in the upper group spent an average of 23·6 per cent of their classroom day on routine whereas teachers in the lower half averaged 44·7 per cent.

Apparently, teachers with higher self-concepts tend to spend less of their day in routine non-thinking activities. The tapes revealed that these teachers appear to delegate the routine activities to individual youngsters, leaving the teacher and class free to pursue thinking-learning activities.

The third analysis was concerned with the amount of classroom time spent in various thinking processes and any possible relationship between the use of these thinking processes and teacher self-concept. Basic rationale would lead one to believe that a teacher's self-concept might affect the kind of thinking she uses. For example, one might expect individuals with stronger self-images to use more evaluative thinking and to feel freer in allowing others to evaluate them. Also, teachers readily admit that when they feel unsure of themselves in a teaching area they stick to memory, convergent thinking and 'right answer' kinds of questions.

Figure 1: *Teacher self-concept and proportion of time teacher talks*

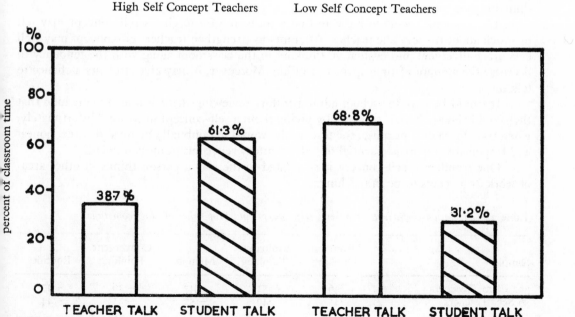

Therefore, a correlational study was employed to investigate the relation between teacher self-concept and the kind of thinking she uses. Correlations were run between the teacher's total self-concept score and the proportion of each thinking process she used as counted on the audio-tapes from her classroom. Data on elementary and secondary teachers were kept separate. These data were collected separately because teachers themselves postulated there would be significant differences between the two. Their rationale grew from the notion that elementary teachers tend to be person-oriented while secondary teachers are more subject-oriented. Results of the correlation study are shown in Table 1.

All results shown in the table are significantly different from zero, meaning that the correlation indicated is highly unlikely to be due to chance fluctuation. Further, the elementary and secondary results are not significantly different from one another; hence the person-oriented versus subject-oriented hypothesis was not substantiated here.

The correlations in Table 1 indicate a positive and rather high relationship between self-concept and the tendency to use divergent and evaluative thinking. The higher the self-concept, the more of these thinking processes a teacher uses. The negative correlations of self-concept with memory and, to a lesser extent, convergent thinking provide evidence that the less positive a teacher's self-concept, the more likely she is to use memory and convergent thinking with her class; also, as shown earlier, she tends to spend more time on routine, non-thinking activities.

The thinking-category data are mutually exclusive, of course, and therefore not independent.

Discussion

All of the investigations of teacher self-concept were found to result in significant differences, except that no significant differences existed between elementary and secondary teachers. The extent of differences in self-concept between individual teachers was great. Important differences were found between a teacher's self-concept and the percentage of classroom time (1) she talks (2) she spends on routine, and (3) she uses various thinking processes.

The evidence seems to indicate that a measure of a teacher's self-concept may tell us much about the way she teaches. Attempts to strengthen teacher self-concept may well encourage divergent and evaluative thinking in the classroom along with the tendency to decrease the amount of time spent in routine. Moreover, it may give students a chance to talk more.

It would be easy for school administrators reviewing these studies to conclude that they could choose 'better' teachers by giving them a self-concept measure. Unfortunately, when used for such a purpose, the test results would undoubtedly be invalid. Free, honest and responsible report is essential to self-inventory self-concept measurement.

One wonders if self-concept is so related to the way a person thinks in other areas of work as it seems to be in teaching.

Table 1: *Correlation coefficients: teacher's self-concept and proportion of classroom time*

Sample	Divergent Thinking	Evaluative Thinking	Memory	Convergent Thinking	Routine
302 Elem. Teachers . . .	·46	·51	−·47	−·26	−·47
56 Sec. Teachers . . .	·41	·49	−·52	−·21	−·44

BIBLIOGRAPHY

ASCHNER, M. J. and GALLAGHER, J. (1962). *A System for Classifying Thought Processes in the Context of Verbal Classroom Interaction*. Champaign, Ill.: University of Illinois Press.

BLOOM, B. (1956). *Taxonomy of Educational Objectives*. New York: David McKay.

CLARK, B. M. and TROWBRIDGE, N. T. (1971). 'Encouraging creativity through in-service teacher education', *J. Res. & Devel. in Educ.*

FITTS, W. (1965). *The Tennessee Self-concept Scale*. Nashville, Tenn.: Counselor Recordings and Tests.

GALLAGHER, J. J. (1960). *Analysis of Research on the Education of Gifted Children*. Springfield, Ill.: Office of the Superintendant of Public Instruction.

GUILFORD, J. P. (1956). 'Structure of the intellect', *Psychol. Bull.*, **53**, 267–93.

PIAGET, J. (1951). *The Psychology of Intelligence*. London: Routledge.

TROWBRIDGE, N. T. (1970). 'The Measurement'. In: ROWSON, J. P. (Ed.), *Impact* **70**. Des Moines, Iowa: Polk County Education Services.

TROWBRIDGE, N. T. (1970). 'Self-concept and socio-economic class', *Psychol. in the Schools*, **7**, 3.

WYLIE, R. C. (1961). *The Self Concept*. Lincoln, Nebraska: University of Nebraska Press.